Current
CONTROVERSIES

◁ **W9-ART-467**

Tariffs and the
Future of Trade

Other Books in the Current Controversies Series

Tariffs and the Future of Trade

Eamon Doyle, Book Editor

GREENHAVEN
PUBLISHING

Published in 2020 by Greenhaven Publishing, LLC
353 3rd Avenue, Suite 255, New York, NY 10010

Cover image: GREG BAKER/AFP/Getty Images

Library of Congress Cataloging-in-Publication Data

Names: Doyle, Eamon, 1988– editor.
Title: Tariffs and the future of trade / Eamon Doyle, book editor.
Description: First edition. | New York : Greenhaven Publishing, 2020. |
 Series: Current controversies | Includes bibliographical references and
 index. | Audience: Grades 9-12.
Identifiers: LCCN 2018061365| ISBN 9781534505452 (library bound) | ISBN
 9781534505469 (pbk.)
Subjects: LCSH: Tariff—Juvenile literature. | Free trade—Juvenile
 literature. | Commercial policy—Juvenile literature. | International
 trade—Juvenile literature.
Classification: LCC HF1713 .T365 2020 | DDC 382/.7—dc23
LC record available at https://lccn.loc.gov/2018061365

Manufactured in the United States of America

Website: http://greenhavenpublishing.com

Contents

Chapter 1: Are Tariffs and Other Protectionist Policies Worth the Risk?

Yes: Aggressive Trade Policies Are a Way to Exert International Influence Without Violence

Chapter 2: Does Free Trade Benefit Investors at the Expense of Workers?

Author and economist William Krist describes how prevailing theories on trade policy have evolved since the era of early capitalist writers like Adam Smith. He also analyzes how modern dynamics in the global economy, including changes to trade agreements, affect domestic labor markets in the United States and around the world.

Yes: Most of the Benefits of Free Trade Are for Business Owners and Consumers

Economists Uri Dadush and William Shaw explore the structural tendencies of globalized capitalism, including how its effects can increase domestic income inequalities while still leveling the field for workers on a global scale.

Originally published by the International Labour Organization (ILO), this viewpoint outlines the risks of globalization from the perspective of working class populations. ILO argues that sustainable economic development on a global scale requires the establishment of basic employment standards and labor norms.

Xavier Devictor summarizes data trends related to opportunity, income, and global free trade. He argues that major disparities exist in the distribution of globalization's rewards, not only between social classes but also between countries, industries, and professions.

No: Free Trade Promotes Economic Growth and Development in All Areas, Including Labor Markets

Analyst Denise Froning argues in favor of free trade and globalization. Her central point is that the interdependence of economic systems across the world ensures a widespread distribution of globalization's benefits, even when its direct effects appear to advantage one group or region over another.

Chapter 3: Does Global Trade Reduce Benefits of a Local Cultural and Economic System?

**Yes: Globalization Has Increased Volatility
and Does Not Serve the Common Good**

This viewpoint, originally published by the World Trade Organization (WTO), looks at the impact of US trade agreements in the late twentieth century and argues that protectionist policies represent a threat to the overall viability of the modern US economy.

Pankaj Ghemawat

In this viewpoint, economist Pankaj Ghemawat suggests that critics of globalization and free trade have exaggerated the impact of globalization on negative economic trends, many of which are caused by a confluence of factors. Ghemawat argues that the complexity of global economics makes it difficult to ascribe such trends to a single factor like trade liberalization.

Michael Matheson Miller

Michael Matheson Miller rejects the notion that liberal trade policies damage the integrity of local cultures. He suggests that a holistic view of economics and culture allows one to see the relationship between these dynamics in terms of evolution rather than conflict.

The World Bank Group

Though originally published in 1987, the long view of global trade presented in this viewpoint remains relevant to this day. It discusses the history of trade liberalization and the positive impacts it had on global prosperity, while also arguing that protectionist policies are ineffective at saving domestic jobs and ultimately harm consumers around the world.

Foreword

"Controversy" is a word that has an undeniably unpleasant connotation. It carries a definite negative charge. Controversy can spoil family gatherings, spread a chill around classroom and campus discussion, inflame public discourse, open raw civic wounds, and lead to the ouster of public officials. We often feel that controversy is almost akin to bad manners, a rude and shocking eruption of that which must not be spoken or thought of in polite, tightly guarded society. To avoid controversy, to quell controversy, is often seen as a public good, a victory for etiquette, perhaps even a moral or ethical imperative.

Yet the studious, deliberate avoidance of controversy is also a whitewashing, a denial, a death threat to democracy. It is a false sterilizing and sanitizing and superficial ordering of the messy, ragged, chaotic, at times ugly processes by which a healthy democracy identifies and confronts challenges, engages in passionate debate about appropriate approaches and solutions, and arrives at something like a consensus and a broadly accepted and supported way forward. Controversy is the megaphone, the speaker's corner, the public square through which the citizenry finds and uses its voice. Controversy is the life's blood of our democracy and absolutely essential to the vibrant health of our society.

Our present age is certainly no stranger to controversy. We are consumed by fierce debates about technology, privacy, political correctness, poverty, violence, crime and policing, guns, immigration, civil and human rights, terrorism, militarism, environmental protection, and gender and racial equality. Loudly competing voices are raised every day, shouting opposing opinions, putting forth competing agendas, and summoning starkly different visions of a utopian or dystopian future. Often these voices attempt to shout the others down; there is precious little listening and considering among the cacophonous din. Yet listening and considering, too, are essential to the health of a democracy. If controversy is democracy's lusty lifeblood, respectful listening and careful thought are its higher faculties, its brain, its conscience.

Current Controversies does not shy away from or attempt to hush the loudly competing voices. It seeks to provide readers with as wide and representative as possible a range of articulate voices on any given controversy of the day, separates each one out to allow it to be heard clearly and fairly, and encourages careful listening to each of these well-crafted, thoughtfully expressed opinions, supplied by some of today's leading academics, thinkers, analysts, politicians, policy makers, economists, activists, change agents, and advocates. Only after listening to a wide range of opinions on an issue, evaluating the strengths and weaknesses of each argument, assessing how well the facts and available evidence mesh with the stated opinions and conclusions, and thoughtfully and critically examining one's own beliefs and conscience can the reader begin to arrive at his or her own conclusions and articulate his or her own stance on the spotlighted controversy.

This process is facilitated and supported in each Current Controversies volume by an introduction and chapter overviews that provide readers with the essential context they need to begin engaging with the spotlighted controversies, with the debates surrounding them, and with their own perhaps shifting or nascent opinions on them. Chapters are organized around several key questions that are answered with diverse opinions representing all points on the political spectrum. In its content, organization, and methodology, readers are encouraged to determine the authors' point of view and purpose, interrogate and analyze the various arguments and their rhetoric and structure, evaluate the arguments' strengths and weaknesses, test their claims against available facts and evidence, judge the validity of the reasoning, and bring into clearer, sharper focus the reader's own beliefs and conclusions and how they may differ from or align with those in the collection or those of classmates.

Research has shown that reading comprehension skills improve dramatically when students are provided with compelling, intriguing, and relevant "discussable" texts. The subject matter of these collections could not be more compelling, intriguing, or urgently relevant to today's students and the world they are poised to inherit. The anthologized articles also provide the basis for stimulating, lively, and passionate classroom debates. Students who are compelled to anticipate objections to their own argument and identify the flaws in those of an opponent read more carefully, think more critically, and steep themselves in relevant context, facts, and information more thoroughly. In short, using discussable text of the kind provided by every single volume in the Current Controversies series encourages close reading, facilitates reading comprehension, fosters research, strengthens critical thinking, and greatly enlivens and energizes classroom discussion and participation. The entire learning process is deepened, extended, and strengthened.

If we are to foster a knowledgeable, responsible, active, and engaged citizenry, we must provide readers with the intellectual, interpretive, and critical-thinking tools and experience necessary to make sense of the world around them and of the all-important debates and arguments that inform it. We must encourage them not to run away from or attempt to quell controversy but to embrace it in a responsible, conscientious, and thoughtful way, to sharpen and strengthen their own informed opinions by listening to and critically analyzing those of others. This series encourages respectful engagement with and analysis of current controversies and competing opinions and fosters a resulting increase in the strength and rigor of one's own opinions and stances. As such, it helps readers assume their rightful place in the public square and provides them with the skills necessary to uphold their awesome responsibility—guaranteeing the continued and future health of a vital, vibrant, and free democracy.

Introduction

Capitalism and free trade represent two of the distinguishing features of the modern world. Prior to the twentieth century, economic power was largely centralized among the nobility and political elite in advanced societies. In this environment, mercantilism stood out as the prevailing economic ideology. The economist William Krist writes:

> In the seventeenth and eighteenth centuries, the predominant thinking was that a successful nation should export more than it imports and that the trade surplus should be used to expand the nation's treasure, primarily gold and silver. This would allow the country to have a bigger and more powerful army and navy and more colonies. Mercantilists believed that governments should promote exports and that governments should control economic activity and place restrictions on imports if needed to ensure an export surplus. Obviously, not all nations could have an export surplus, but mercantilists believed this was the goal and that successful nations would gain at the expense of those less successful. Ideally, a nation would export finished goods and import raw materials, under mercantilist theory, thereby maximizing domestic employment. [1]

This began to change in the late nineteenth century as the industrial revolution unfolded and modern global capitalism took hold. In the twentieth century, liberal economics would largely supplant the mercantilist perspective on trade and economics.

Since the Second World War, the major Western powers—including the United States, Britain, France, and Germany—have defined themselves in large measure by a commitment to economic and political liberalism. In the context of international affairs, this commitment has expressed itself in the global trade system and the network of capitalist institutions that bind these countries and their populations together.

This arrangement has a number of economic and political benefits, as the British economist Alexander Tziamalis explains:

> Economic theory stipulates that free trade makes everything cheaper and improves the quality of products, directly benefiting everyone. The argument goes that if each country focused and specialised on what they do best or cheapest, they would produce better quality or cheaper products. These could then be traded between countries, making every consumer happier ... Free trade has lifted whole countries out of poverty. It can bring a lot of income from abroad and can push businesses towards continuous investment, hard effort and innovation to expand their international market-share ... In addition, free trade strengthens the links between countries, boosts economic co-operation and, the argument goes, makes wars less likely—after all, it's not wise to invade your customers and suppliers. This was a fundamental reason for the creation of the European Economic Community, the precursor to the EU, shortly after World War II. [2]

But despite widespread agreement among economists on the benefits of global free trade, there are a number of potential drawbacks as well. For instance, global financial systems are vulnerable to increased volatility when the collateral effects of local events reverberate around the globe. Many social scientists also worry about the effects of commercial and economic homogenization on non-Western societies. Consider the following argument from a paper published by the United Nations Educational, Scientific, and Cultural Organization (UNESCO):

> In the contemporary world—characterized as it is by space-time compression linked to the speed of new communication and transportation technologies, and by the growing complexity of social interactions and the increasing overlap of individual and collective identities—cultural diversity has become a key concern, amid accelerating globalization processes, as a resource to be preserved and as a lever for sustainable development.[3]

In addition to the type of cultural concerns outlined by UNESCO, recent developments have led to more basic questions about the economics of global free trade.

As globalization has progressed, its effects have become more widespread and radical. Over the past several decades, for instance, computer technology has occupied an increasingly central role in the business and financial world. This has had a number of wide-ranging effects, but perhaps most importantly it has increased the pace and the scope of business and commercial evolution. As a consequence, labor market in sectors like manufacturing and accounting have experienced tremendous upheaval:

> The forces of globalization have been associated with both rising living standards and a deterioration in income distribution in advanced countries: Low-skilled wages have remained flat or even declined, while high-skilled wages have increased sharply … Inequality also has increased in many developing countries … As in advanced countries, openness to trade and foreign investment have increased the relative return to skilled labor and capital, while reducing the relative return to unskilled labor. Indeed, some analyses find that trade and financial liberalization episodes, or openness in general, have contributed to worsening income inequality, at least in the middle-income countries.[4]

The general sense of economic insecurity that these dynamics have produced, particularly among working class populations, has contributed to growing suspicions about the benefits of economic liberalism. In this context, protectionist ideals have experienced a resurgence on the political stage. Examples of this resurgence include the 2016 Brexit referendum in the UK and President Donald Trump's significant tariffs on international goods in 2018.

We are clearly witnessing a major evolution in the way that people around the world perceive and interpret the nature of global capitalism. This process of evolution comes with both risks and opportunities, which is why it is critical that policymakers and citizens attend to the enormous complexity of these issues. *Current Controversies: Tariffs and the Future of Trade* examines trade policies of the past and present to give a better sense of what the future may hold.

Notes

1. "Trade Agreements and Economic Theory," by William Krist, Johns Hopkins University Press.

2. "Explainer: What Is Protectionism and Could It Benefit the US Economy?" by Alexander Tziamalis, *The Conversation*, March 1, 2017. https://theconversation .com/explainer-what-is-protectionism-and-could-it-benefit-the-us -economy-73706.

3. "Investing in Cultural Diversity and Intercultural Dialogue," UNESCO Publications, 2007.

4. "Globalization, Labor Markets, and Inequality," by Uri Dadush and William Shaw, Carnegie Endowment for International Peace, February 2, 2012.

CHAPTER 1

Are Tariffs and Other Protectionist Policies Worth the Risk?

What Are Tariffs, What Is a Trade War, and Why Are They Important?

Michael Johnson

Michael Johnson is a British consultant who works with governments around the world on trade policy and related issues. He was a senior official in the United Kingdom's Department of Trade and Industry.

P resident Donald Trump has signed an order for special tariffs of 25% on imports into the United States of foreign steel, and 10% on aluminium. He openly says that this could lead to a trade war, which he could easily win. But what exactly is a trade war?

There is no set definition. In the 17th century, England and Holland fought actual wars for domination of European and colonial trade. In the 1930s, responding to the world economic slump, major trading countries tried to protect industries and jobs from competition by imposing steep tariffs and other restrictions on imports. When we talk nowadays about trade wars, we mean aggressive tit-for-tat use of tariffs and other administrative actions affecting trade.

What Are Tariffs and Why Do They Matter?

Import tariffs, also called customs duties, are a basic tool of trade policy. They are financial charges on imported goods levied by governments and collected by national customs authorities. Their purpose is to protect domestic producers from competition from cheaper imports; often at the same time they raise government revenue and prevent disruption from unfair trade practices. Usually the charge is a percentage of the consignment value, but sometimes it is a "specific" duty, ie a fixed sum per unit of quantity, weight or volume.

"Here Is What You Need to Know about the Risks of a US Trade War," by Michael Johnson, World Economic Forum, March 9, 2018. Reprinted by permission.

All trading countries base their tariffs on a so-called "harmonized system", which has 99 chapters covering more than 5,000 individual product descriptions and many subdivisions. Item by item, governments apply their own chosen rates of tariff (or no tariff). Very rarely, a government may apply a tariff to exports of an item which is a valuable national resource, in order to deter exports and maintain domestic supply.

How Do Tariffs Work in Customs Unions and Free Trade Areas?

A customs union is a treaty-based grouping of countries which remove tariffs and other barriers to trade (such as quotas or differing trade procedures) between themselves. All apply the same tariffs and procedures to trade with non-members (the fullest current example is the European Union). In a free trade area the countries remove tariffs and other trade barriers among themselves, but each is free to apply its own independent regime to trade with non-members. World Trade Organisation (WTO) rules require in both cases that the participant countries remove "substantially all" trade restrictions between themselves, which in practice means 90% or more.

Can Governments Use Special Tariffs to Protect Domestic Industry and Trade?

Yes, within strict limits laid down by the WTO. Where a domestic industry complains of unfair and damaging competition from a foreign company selling a product into the market at artificially low prices or below cost ("dumping"), or from a foreign government unfairly subsidising exports, the government of the importing country may investigate the complaint. If it determines that dumping and/or subsidisation are taking place and causing or threatening injury to the complaining industry, then so-called "anti-dumping" or "countervailing" duties may be imposed on the imports up to a level sufficient to counteract the margin of dumping or subsidy.

Often the threat of an investigation may be enough to remedy the abuse. Alternatively, instead of applying a duty the investigating government may accept an undertaking from the exporting company or government to increase prices of the items concerned.

There is another WTO provision which is sometimes used where a sudden surge of imports appears to be damaging a domestic industry. The importing government may investigate the complaint and if it is justified, may impose for a limited time a "safeguard" in the form of special import tariffs or quotas to counteract the surge.

But Isn't That Just What President Trump Is Doing?

No, only in the recent case where Boeing complained that the Bombardier aircraft company was being unfairly subsidized by the Canadian and UK governments to sell small airliners into the US. The Administration found that subsidization was taking place and proposed 300% countervailing duties on the imports. However, they could not be implemented because the independent US International Trade Commission, which is responsible for determining whether or not injury is taking place or is threatened, ruled that Boeing was not injured, since it did not make the class of planes in question.

Back in January 2018, and in response to complaints by major US manufacturers, the US imposed anti-dumping duties on imports of solar panels and washing machines. The structure of these duties is complex, but they may in some cases be as high as 30% for solar panels, and for washing machines 50%.

On the new steel tariffs, the Administration carried out an investigation of steel imports under a quite different provision, namely the US Trade Expansion Act of 1962, which permits the Administration to act against imports of "any article" which appear to endanger US national security. WTO rules do permit member governments to take trade defensive action in the event of threats to national security.

In the steel case, the US invokes the national security defence on the ground that a viable indigenous steel industry is vital to the entire economy. But it is unlikely that this let-out can be stretched, as the US has done, to justify imposition of tariffs covering every class of a particular commodity, especially one as multifarious as steel. That issue can only be resolved, as it probably will be, by action under the WTO disputes settlement system.

In the case of aluminium, the US has carried out no formal investigation at all. The Administration has simply imposed a blanket 10% duty. This is not permissible under WTO rules, and the US Administration has offered no justification for its action apart from general references to national security.

So Shouldn't Other Countries Affected by the US Tariffs on Steel and Aluminium Retaliate Against US Trade?

That would be a big step towards unleashing a "trade war". The President of the European Commission initially spoke about retaliation, but the US' trading partners, including China, are now being more circumspect. Retaliation, whether in the form of special duties or quotas, would in the absence of due process also be against WTO rules; and it would hurt industries, traders and consumers on both sides.

This happened back in the 1980s when the European Community first banned imports of US hormone-fed beef in a dispute that still drags on today. Then the US imposed retaliatory trade sanctions against imports of some important European products. The European Community got as far as discussing a list of US products for counter-retaliation, though that was never activated. The right way to deal with the current US action is through the established, and effective, WTO disputes system.

What Is the US Up To on Trade?

On present form, "America First" is a threat to the entire basis of the multilateral trading system. At the World Economic Forum in

January, US Commerce Secretary Wilbur Ross was challenged about whether the US was risking the launch of a trade war. He said that US actions on trade were aimed to fix "incorrect policy decisions" which had been taken under a post-World War Two system (meaning the system of rules developed under the General Agreement on Tariffs and Trade and now the WTO) that was no longer appropriate. The US did not intend to abrogate its leadership role in world trade, but the basis must be "more fair and equitable", and the US would no longer be "a sucker or a patsy" on trade. On a different interpretation however, America does seem to be stepping back from its history as a main driver of the open international trading system.

Who Suffers from Trade Wars?

We all do. Manufacturers in producing countries lose output, profits and jobs. Ancillary traders and services like shippers, financiers, insurers and importers lose turnover. Consumers in importing countries face reduced availability of goods, and higher prices. Governments suffer loss of revenue because of reduced trade volumes. When in the 1930s major industrialised countries tried to protect their domestic industries through aggressive use of import tariffs or other trade restrictions, the result was a drop of around half in the volume of world trade, which contributed to mass unemployment and impoverishment.

In the modern world of globalised production and value chains there would be severe risk of disruption of component supply lines, with knock-on effects on manufacturing, output, costs and employment.

What's Likely to Happen Next?

It's hard to say. The Trump Administration is determined to persist in rebalancing the international trading system more in the US' favour. We don't know what might be the next target for protectionism, following the attempted action on aircraft subsidies (though that failed), and the tariffs on solar panels, washing machines, steel and aluminium.

The steel case is important to producers all over the world who export to the US. If affected exporting countries prefer to maintain the moral high ground, their recourse will certainly be a challenge in the WTO, which could cover the aluminium tariffs too. But that could take a year or more to settle if the initial dispute panel findings were referred (as they certainly would be) to appeal. Meanwhile the US looks like [it is] getting away with protectionist actions, so long as its major trading partners, above all China and the EU, regard the risk of a full-on trade war as the greater and more damaging threat.

It May Not Be the Answer Today, but Protectionism Has Worked in the Past

Zhang Jun

Zhang Jun is director of the Shanghai-based China Center for Economic Studies. He is also Dean of the School of Economics at Fudan University and serves on the special advisory committee to the Shanghai municipal government.

US President Donald Trump's announced plans to target China with trade tariffs represent a significant departure from his predecessors' approach. China is now seen primarily as an economic adversary, rather than an economic partner. That may be a difference of degree rather than kind: Trump's policies are the culmination of a decade of US trade frustration.

The sources of US frustration are well known. Since joining the World Trade Organization in 2001, China has been accused of failing to meet its market-access obligations, and even of having regressed in some areas. Moreover, China is believed to have long used state intervention, including industrial policy, to limit US businesses and investment in the domestic market, while enabling Chinese enterprises to achieve rapid technological progress.

More fundamentally, however, the US is concerned that China's rapid economic development now poses a real challenge to America's global influence. This has fueled a sense that China must be "contained." In Trump's view, part of the solution is trade protectionism.

In the 1980s, protectionist US policies successfully contained the growth of Japan, which, like China today, maintained a large trade surplus with the US. But those policies' success was rooted partly in Japan's problematic policy choices, including slow fiscal and monetary responses. In order to reduce the bilateral

"China's Smart Trade Moves," by Zhang Jun, Project Syndicate, May 28, 2018. Reprinted by permission.

trade surplus, Japan introduced so-called voluntary export restraints, which hollowed out its real economy, while providing excessive protection to its non-tradable sectors. The result was a decades-long recession.

But trade patterns have changed so much since the 1980s, particularly owing to the emergence of regional and global supply chains, that the very notion of a bilateral trade imbalance—one of the main sticking points for Trump—seems outdated. After all, the added value China actually derives from its exports is not nearly as large as its trade surplus.

In fact, over the last decade, China's global current-account surplus has shrunk at an unprecedented rate, falling from 10% of GDP in 2007 to a mere 1.4% today. Meanwhile, there has been little change in the US trade imbalance, indicating that America's massive deficit is not China's fault at all. In fact, the blame lies squarely with US macroeconomic realities, namely a low rate of domestic saving and a high rate of federal borrowing, which Trump's tax cuts will cause to increase further.

China recognizes the absurdity of the Trump administration's obsession with forcing it to reduce the bilateral trade surplus. But it also knows that a trade war would not be good for anyone. To ease trade frictions, unlike Japan's voluntary export restraints, China's leaders have promised to increase imports and open up the domestic market, with President Xi Jinping predicting $8 trillion worth of merchandise imports within the next five years.

This is a smart move, and not just because it will help appease the US, as well as European countries that have complained about limited access to the Chinese market, not to mention international financial institutions. As underscored in a joint statement of the US and China regarding trade consultations, "significantly" increased Chinese purchases of foreign—in particular, US—goods and services will also enable the country "to meet the growing consumption needs of the Chinese people and the need for high-quality economic development."

China imported $2 trillion worth of goods in 2017, of which consumer goods accounted for only 8.8%. Expanding the share of consumer goods might significantly improve the welfare of Chinese citizens, who, because of existing tariffs and non-tariff barriers, now often travel abroad to make purchases. In fact, international purchases by Chinese are now equivalent to the value of all of the consumer goods China currently imports, even without taking into account fast-rising online overseas purchases.

Shifting those purchases to China would help propel the shift toward a more consumption-driven economy, particularly as the middle class—and its purchasing power—grows. The impact would be even greater if US and European countries responded to Chinese calls to export high-tech products more freely.

Similarly, greater openness to investment is crucial for China as it seeks to ensure continued technological progress. As it stands, even if China's economy is the same size as America's, China will maintain a competitive advantage in manufacturing, because its *per capita* GDP is only one-quarter that of the US.

Yet China remains in a low position on global value chains, despite recent improvements. And, so far, its technological advancement has depended largely on greater openness to direct investment, which has supported progress in research, development, and application of advanced technologies.

If China is to continue upgrading its economy, this process must continue, supported by initiatives to promote entrepreneurship and protect intellectual property rights. Fortunately, China knows this well. The authorities are hoping for foreign direct investment of $600 billion in the coming five years, and expect Chinese outward direct investment to reach $750 billion five years later.

Already, China is backing up its words with action. To promote expanded consumer imports, the country will hold its first import expo in Shanghai in November. To spur financial investment, China will raise foreign-ownership limits to 51% within three years, on the path toward ultimately removing restrictions altogether. By 2022, it will scrap foreign ownership limits on local auto firms, boosting companies like Tesla, which could then fully own a subsidiary in China.

To be sure, more must be done, and China needs to go further to clear institutional barriers to manufacturing and financial reforms. But China has already shown itself to be handling US trade pressure in a more savvy way than Japan did in the 1980s. Indeed, far from laying the groundwork for a protracted recession, China's response—increasing imports and accelerating domestic structural reforms—will support high-quality long-term growth.

Protectionism and Economic Theory

Alexander Tziamalis

Alexander Tziamalis is a British economist and social scientist currently serving as senior lecturer in economics at Sheffield Hallam University. Prior to his academic career, he was an analyst in the UK Civil Service.

The largest economy on the planet is quickly moving to a protectionist stance in its international trade. US president, Donald Trump, has spoken of withdrawing from the Trans-Pacific Partnership trade deal signed by his predecessor Barack Obama; renegotiating or abandoning the NAFTA trade deal with Mexico and Canada; imposing a 35% tax on every car imported to the US, and even threatening China with a 45% tax on its exports to the US. This could have important ramifications for the US and other world economies.

A protectionist policy is any policy that provides an unfair advantage to a home industry versus the international competition. The practice has a long history in economics. Mercantilism—where countries augmented their power through regulation that favoured their own economies—was prevalent until the 18th century. But, with trade as one of the engines of economic growth in the 19th and 20th centuries, free trade for all became the benchmark and the goal. And the US was at the forefront of establishing bodies to promote and regulate international trade such as the GATT and its successor, the World Trade Organisation.

Yet forms of protectionism are still used by most states today. The European Union subsidises its own farmers and bans imports of cheap agricultural products from outside the EU. China's currency is artificially low, making its exports cheaper—long the source of friction between it and the US. And Japan helped its industries develop with cheap loans, as well as imposing heavy tariffs on imports, forbidding international investors from buying national companies and even launching local campaigns to persuade its population to buy Japanese products instead of imported goods. To be fair, Japan has now lifted most of these measures, but it only did so when its products had become highly competitive anyway.

The Theory

Economic theory stipulates that free trade makes everything cheaper and improves the quality of products, directly benefiting everyone. This stems from the fact that different countries have different production strengths. These could be a cheap workforce, technological expertise, geography or a rare resource.

The argument goes that if each country focused and specialised on what they do best or cheapest, they would produce better quality or cheaper products. These could then be traded between countries, making every consumer happier. It's a similar principle to everyone specialising in one career and then trading things we need, rather than trying to produce everything ourselves.

Free trade has lifted whole countries out of poverty. It can bring a lot of income from abroad and can push businesses towards continuous investment, hard effort and innovation to expand their international market-share. This also applies to businesses that do not export, but now need to keep their prices low and their quality high to beat the incoming competition.

In addition, free trade strengthens the links between countries, boosts economic co-operation and, the argument goes, makes wars less likely—after all, it's not wise to invade your customers and suppliers. This was a fundamental reason for the creation of the European Economic Community, the precursor to the EU, shortly after World War II.

When Protectionism Is a Good Idea

There are some important benefits to protectionism, though. As early as 1817, the founder of free trade theory in economics, David Ricardo, recognised that the outcome of free trade may well be to strengthen states with the production advantage and lead to job losses for others. In situations where capital is mobile, and without any barriers to the flow of people and investment, all production could well move to one part of the world—sound familiar?

Protectionism is also a good idea when dealing with infant industries. It gives precious time to a company to invest in its production facilities, personnel skills and gain the local consumer's trust before the national market finally opens to international competitors. The success of Japanese, South Korean and Chinese industrialisation is partly due to the fact that these countries shielded their industries in their infant stages, allowing them time to grow and strengthen before they had to compete with the industries of the West.

This argument can also be extended to important industries that are experiencing temporary problems. The Obama administration's decision to bail out the US car industry in the wake of the 2008 financial crisis followed this logic.

Another strong argument in favour of protectionism follows the logic of Game Theory. If your competitor countries are going to offer protection to their industries anyway, then you should offer protection to your industries, too. For example, if the US government is indirectly subsidising the American airplane manufacturer Boeing, then EU countries have a strong case to retaliate and consider subsidising the European company Airbus as well. If they don't, then Boeing will eventually gain a much higher market share which, in turn, might push Airbus out of business altogether.

A Gamble for Trump that Could Pay Off

So there's certainly a case for protectionism, but Trump's proposed policies are also a gamble. The obvious danger is that if Trump's policies are enacted in full, they will substantially increase prices in the US.

For example, the car manufacturer Ford claims that if it moved every stage of its production to the US, then some of its cars would be considerably more expensive. Tariffs on imports would mean that all the goods imported from Asia, Latin America and Europe would be more expensive, too.

Faced with the debilitating effect of rising inflation, the central bank of the US, the Federal Reserve, might have to increase interest rates more aggressively to limit the damage. Higher interest rates will then further reduce the buying power of the American consumer and reduce inward investment. Plus, it is also likely that US trading partners will retaliate in kind, to the detriment of US exports and the companies that manufacture them, further hurting demand for American products.

The key to success lies in the confidence and expectations of businesses and consumers. If people believe that Trump's policies are geared towards economic growth then, as a self-fulfilling prophecy, they will bring this growth with investment and spending. A possible early indication of this sentiment could be the rise of the Dow Jones stock index following Trump's election and an unprecedented surge in economic optimism.

If American companies believe that the new policies will boost consumption of American products, rather than imports, then they have an incentive to invest in their production and hire locally. Plus, if Trump's threat to impose huge tariffs is believed, many foreign companies that currently produce outside the US will have an incentive to relocate within its borders. Employment levels, salaries, spending and confidence by consumers and businesses will go up further, triggering even more inward investment.

The most likely way that Trump's policies could benefit the US economy, though, is simply by posing a credible threat to US trading partners. Once the outrage against his protectionist threat subsides, a number of countries will be happier to lift their own forms of protectionism against American products and sign trade deals more favourable for US exports. American governments have long tried to persuade China to allow its currency to appreciate; now Trump intends to strong-arm them.

International Strategy and the Viability of Tariffs

Evan Horowitz

Evan Horowitz is a journalist whose work focuses on political and economic issues. His writing has appeared in the Boston Globe, *the* Washington Post, *the* Chicago Tribune, MSN, RealClearPolitics, *and* FiveThirtyEight.

Republicans are in revolt. Economists on the left and right are deeply skeptical. President Trump's top economic adviser resigned rather than be party to it. The culprit: tariffs, and specifically the president's decision to slap duties on imported steel (25 percent) and aluminum (10 percent).

Though they are widely vilified, tariffs actually can work, providing protection for a few vulnerable companies, safeguarding entire industries, maybe even encouraging a wholesale reassessment of what counts as fair trade. Tariffs also come with considerable costs and risks, however, and making the gambit work requires a well-defined goal and a winning strategy. And it's not clear that Trump has the detailed plan needed to make this gamble pay off.

One early estimate of Trump's plans, for example, uses a variant of a well-respected model to project that the tariffs would eliminate five jobs for every one they save, because the help they offer steel producers is more than offset by the elevated prices that users of manufactured steel, like car manufacturers, wind up having to pay. This is often a risk with tariffs: By raising the price of imported goods, tariffs strain the budgets of companies—and consumers—who buy those goods. In addition, tariffs can provoke an escalating trade war in which foreign countries who resent the new border tax fight back by implementing protectionist measures of their own.

"Tariffs Can Work—When They're Part of a Plan," by Evan Horowitz, ABC News Internet Ventures, March 13, 2018. Reprinted by permission.

But these risks don't mean tariffs are doomed to fail; they just require a long-term goal that justifies the short-term cost in jobs and dollars—and a way to reach it.

This kind of targeted tariff helped save Harley Davidson, for example. In the early 1980s, the company was losing market share to smaller, more affordable imports from Japan. Bankruptcy seemed a real possibility until President Ronald Reagan agreed to introduce a severe protective tariff.

Deliberately designed to be fast-acting and short-lived, the tariff started at a steep 49.4 percent before gradually falling back to the normal 4.4 percent rate over the course five years. In the end, it didn't take that long for Harley Davidson to reorganize its operations, fix manufacturing problems and return to profitability. By year four, they felt secure enough that they actually asked for the tariffs to be lifted early (presumably because the tax had already fallen dramatically and because a show of strength was good PR).

To some observers, that turnaround might still count as a failure because the company recovered not on its own but with the help of regulations that, by their very nature, interfere with the free market, limiting consumer choices and putting upward pressure on prices. But clearly the tariffs accomplished their basic goal, blunting competition from Japan in order to give an iconic US company breathing room to catch up.

Now consider a broader example of tariffs in action, namely the heavily protectionist world of European agriculture. The EU operates under an integrated set of policies designed to ensure a decent standard of living for Europe's farmers while also guaranteeing a reliable supply of food for European citizens. Among those policies are direct payments to farmers, funding for rural development—and also tariffs, including some tariffs that bite deeply into the pockets of US farmers. When sending goods to Europe, American farmers face an average tariff of 13.7 percent, or nearly three times what EU farmers face when exporting their products to the US.

All this special treatment for native agriculture comes at a serious cost, of course: Over a third of the EU budget goes to support the roughly 5 percent of citizens involved in farming, which is money that can't be used for other urban or industrial priorities. But what really matters is whether Europeans think these costs are outweighed by the benefits that come with tariffs and other agricultural supports. And in a recent Eurobarometer poll, 52 percent of respondents said they "totally agree" or "tend to agree" that the EU should have trade barriers for agricultural products, compared to 34 percent who disagreed.

Which brings us back to Trump's decision to impose a 25 percent tariff on steel imports from outside North America and a 10 percent levy on aluminum. Here, too, the defining question shouldn't be, "What will it cost?" but rather, "What's the underlying goal, and can it be achieved at a reasonable cost?"

The chosen goal might be quite narrow, along the lines Trump himself outlined when he signed the tariff proclamations last Thursday: "A strong steel and aluminum industry are vital to our national security." Ensuring that the US can produce enough steel to keep building planes and ships in the event of a military emergency seems like a tailored and well-defined objective, not unlike the aim of the tightly targeted Harley Davidson tariff.

But narrow efforts aren't always the most successful. The last time the US imposed steel tariffs in an attempt to bolster the industry, under President George W. Bush, the real-world effects proved rather meager. Imports did decline, but seven US steel companies still went bankrupt and the number of workers in the industry seems to have dropped. Partly, this may be because the tariffs didn't last long enough to allow for the kind of restructuring that US steel mills really needed; they were lifted within two years, after the World Trade Organization ruled them illegal. But it's also possible the industry needed more help than tariffs alone could provide as a result of high pension costs and a history of inadequate investment.

With the virtue of hindsight, it seems like the time was ripe during Bush's presidency to pursue a bigger goal: not just helping America's struggling steel industry but helping many US industries fight off the full force of what's sometimes called the "China shock"—the sudden rise in Chinese imports of all kinds after the country joined the WTO and gained broader access to US markets. Between 2000 and 2007, America lost about a million manufacturing jobs, affecting industries well beyond steel. A more ambitious plan—one that included steel tariffs alongside other protections and supports—might have helped defend US industries across the board.

Trump may indeed have something bolder in mind, in which case steel and aluminum tariffs may merely be the opening move. At times, he seems ready to embrace a widening trade war, saying that if Europe retaliates against the steel imports, the US could impose a new tax on EU cars. And during his campaign, he floated the far more disruptive possibility of a 45 percent tariff on Chinese imports.

But if the goal is indeed grander—a realignment in global trade that opens space for more US exports and US manufacturing jobs—then tariffs alone probably won't suffice. Remember that to build a unified agricultural support system, the EU created a complex package of tariffs, subsidies, regulations and rural development aid that all operate in concert.

To ignite a renaissance of US manufacturing, a lot of other things would have to change: The dollar would probably need to fall further, which would help spur exports; countries like China and Germany would have to start saving less and spending more, thus creating more demand for foreign goods, including those made in America; and the US would likely have to pare back its own appetite for imports, including getting Americans to save more money.

Whatever the objective, it needs to be paired with the appropriate tactics. For some goals, tariffs make sense, even if they do come with costs. Ultimately, the only way to assess Trump's tariff plans is not with a ledger comparing the boon for steel producers against the cost for steel users, but by identifying the broader goal—and seeing whether it gets met.

The Potential Hazards of a Trade War Between the United States and China

Linda Yueh

Linda Yueh is a writer, broadcaster, and economist. She currently serves as an adjunct professor of economics at London Business School and editor of the Routledge Economic Growth and Development *book series. As a broadcaster, she fronted the BBC TV series "The New Middle Class" and "Working Lives."*

The tit-for-tat exchange of tariffs between the United States and China gives the impression the world's two biggest economies are headed down the road towards a trade war, which would have hugely damaging economic consequences. But this could be averted if they continue quiet backroom discussions to open up their markets, particularly China's.

The US imposition of tariffs on a range of Chinese imports—which amounts to a tax on imported goods—is the first step in a series of measures announced by the Trump administration. So far, China has responded by announcing tariffs on US imports. The next stage would be for the US to restrict Chinese investment into America.

Presumably, if this happens, then China would respond in kind. In other words, the tensions between the US and China could go beyond taxes and directly disrupt global supply chains as investment is targeted.

Any disruption to supply and distribution chains, which are a key part of world trade, could have a lasting impact. In the worst-case scenario, companies may have to relocate factories or distribution centres. Investment decisions affect employment and taxes raised, and are in some ways more disruptive than tariffs, which can be reversed more easily.

"How a US-China Trade War Would Hurt Us All," by Linda Yueh, Guardian News and Media Limited, April 5, 2018. Reprinted by permission.

This escalation would be damaging for the US and Chinese economies since global companies, such as Apple, invest in both countries. This would affect not only US businesses but also American consumers. Retailers such as Walmart import goods from China, so prices would go up and living standards would be squeezed. And since US goods are sold worldwide, if they are reliant on parts from China, consumers here in the UK and in the rest of the world would also be affected. The same applies to Chinese consumers and producers, particularly since about half of Chinese exports are made by enterprises with foreign investors.

The US is targeting hi-tech manufacturers to disrupt President Xi's flagship industrial strategy, the Made in China 2025 plan, which seeks to make Chinese manufacturing globally competitive by introducing more artificial intelligence and automation. The ability of emerging economies such as China to "catch up" with rich economies depends on their being able to access and adapt the best technology in the world. This lies at the heart of the problem. The US has launched these trade measures in retaliation for China's poor record on intellectual property rights protection, which includes requiring foreign companies to transfer their technology as a condition of investing in China.

So, there is a lot at stake for both countries. But a trade war wouldn't result in better protection of US technology or give American firms better access to Chinese markets. Nor would it help China invest in America. A perennial Chinese complaint is that its companies are blocked, particularly in the technology sector, which is crucial for its economic growth. After an initial round of tariffs on steel and aluminium was unveiled, US and Chinese officials met to discuss ways to open markets wider and create a more level playing field. Opening up China would improve the US trade position. After all, its huge trade deficit could be reduced either by cutting back on imports—or, a much better option, expanding exports.

China may be reluctant to open up its relatively closed markets to foreign competition. It firmly believes its industries need protection against the dominance of multinational companies. But it has some of the biggest companies in the world, such as Alibaba, Huawei, and Tencent. And more competition may well improve China's growth prospects by increasing productivity, especially in sectors where there are less efficient state-owned enterprises.

But far from the US and China coming to the table and forging an agreement to open up trade, more rounds of trade barriers could be announced with growing economic damage and no resolution in sight. President Trump may even show his dissatisfaction with the body that oversees international trade, the World Trade Organisation, which he has described as a "disaster," and pull America out. That would potentially overturn the whole worldwide trading system with dire consequences. So it's critical that a US-China trade war is avoided at all costs.

There Is No Upside to Engaging in a Trade War

Robert Higgs

Robert Higgs currently serves as Editor at Large for the Independent Review. *He has taught economics at the University of Washington and Seattle University, and has spent time as a visiting scholar at Oxford University and Stanford University.*

It is no surprise that President Trump's trade war has many supporters. An understanding of the law of comparative advantage has never been a prominent feature of people's knowledge in the USA or anywhere else. And special interests have honed their propaganda over centuries of angling for the use of government power to protect them from foreign competition, maneuvering to pick the pockets of consumers in their own country.

But even as Trump spouts venerable fallacies to justify and seek support for his destructive trade policies and related *ad hoc* actions, he and his supporters have sometimes offered a strange defense of their tactics: they purport to be seeking, at the end of the game, universal free trade, a world in which all countries have abandoned tariffs, quotas, subsidies, and other government intrusions in international exchange. In Wilsonian terms, they claim to be waging the trade war to end all trade wars. The idea is that by raising US tariffs, they will induce other governments to lower and ultimately eliminate their own.

Of course, this rationale may be nothing more than wily claptrap, tossed out as a rhetorical bone to Republicans who favor freer trade. The administration's actions to date certainly give no indication that it is aiming at global free trade. On the contrary. So the Wilsonian gambit may consist of nothing but hot air.

"No, This Won't Be a 'Trade War to End All Trade Wars,'" by Robert Higgs, Foundation for Economic Education, August 1, 2018. https://fee.org/articles/no-this-wont-be-a-trade-war-to-end-all-trade-wars. Licensed under CC BY 4.0.

But if Trump and his trade advisers actually take this tactic seriously, they are deluding themselves.

You Can't "Win" a Trade War

First, and surely obviously, US tariff increases will not induce other governments to lower their own, but to raise them, as the EU, China, Mexico, Canada, and other trading partners have already demonstrated. That's why it's called a trade war—because the "enemy" shoots back. History has shown repeatedly, most notably in the early 1930s, in the wake of the Smoot-Hawley Tariff Act of 1930, that such trade wars only spiral downward, choking off more and more trade, despoiling the international division of labor in accordance with comparative advantage, and thereby diminishing real income in all the trading countries.

Second, the prospect of the US government's ever abandoning tariffs is slim to none. Tariffs are the classic example of government interventions with concentrated benefits and dispersed costs. This character makes them attract great support from protected special interests and little opposition from the general public—including other producers—when they are enacted or extended. They are easy for politicians to put in place and diabolically difficult for anyone to eliminate. Although the costs are great—much greater than the benefits for the economy as a whole—hardly anyone's costs are great enough to justify mounting a potent political attack on the tariffs.

People who get tariffs put in place to protect them in the first place are well positioned to marshal strong opposition to any political attempt to eliminate these taxes on consumers who buy from competing, foreign suppliers. Consumers rarely know anything about why foreign goods are priced as they are, and producers, in general, are usually not affected enough by tariffs on imported raw materials and components to justify well-funded politicking against them.

Third, even if the trade-war tactic eventually gave rise to a general abandonment of tariffs and other trade restrictions, this outcome would not necessarily mean that the trade war had been a win-win conflict. Of course, a completely free-trading world would be a wonderful, highly beneficial situation, but the question would remain: were the benefits of attaining this result by means of a trade war great enough to justify bearing that war's undeniable costs?

A Trade War, Like All Wars, Comes with Casualties

And make no mistake: this trade war is already proving highly disruptive and destructive. Firms unable to sell to their usual customers abroad are reducing production and laying off workers; firms faced with much higher costs of obtaining foreign raw materials and components for their products are acting likewise.

Moreover, the uncertainty about what the president will do next in conducting his allegedly good war is weighing heavily on entrepreneurs and managers, who are reacting normally to such uncertainty by hunkering down, delaying or canceling investments and new hiring. The greater the uncertainty, the greater the economic paralysis. Back in the 1930s, such regime uncertainty played a major role in prolonging the Great Depression.

Fourth, as trade and trade-related income decline because of the US trade war and other countries' reactions to it, even US and foreign firms whose products may not have been subjected to increased tariffs or other restrictions will suffer, simply because a world with reduced income will demand fewer imports in general. A trade war makes the whole world less efficient; the world economy as a whole produces less output and pays out less income to the producers than it otherwise would. Poorer people make poorer customers for all US firms that sell abroad and for all foreign firms that sell in the USA.

The foregoing considerations are only a few of the many that weigh against the initiation and continuation of a trade war. Trump says such wars are easy to win. In this regard, he apparently doesn't even understand what winning means. The supposition that such a war can be won is a delusion. A trade war may serve Trump's political ambitions by appealing to supporters ignorant of economics and easily bamboozled by anything wrapped in the flag, but the idea of a win-win trade war is the height of folly so far as economic rationality is concerned—not to mention its further suppression of economic liberties already being crushed by taxes and regulations. In fact, the only way to win a trade war is not to fight one.

The Cost of a Large-Scale Trade War for the Global Economy

Manoj Joshi

Manoj Joshi is an Indian historian and journalist. He is a distinguished fellow at the New Delhi-based Observer Research Foundation and his writing has appeared in publications including India Today, *the* Times of India, *and* Mail Today.

The trade war has begun. The US began implementing 25% tariffs on $34 billion worth of goods from the morning of July 6. US tariffs on Chinese imports include semi-conductor chips assembled in China, plastics, dairy equipment, motor vehicles, electrical equipment, oil and gas drilling platform parts, chemicals and lubricants. Earlier, it had put tariffs on washing machines, solar panels, steel and aluminum.

In retaliation, Beijing has hit the US with retaliatory tariffs on 545 products, targeting goods produced in states that voted for Donald Trump in 2016—products like soybean, beef, fish, fruits, vegetables, dairy products, bourbon, cotton, tobacco and motor vehicles.

This is said to be the biggest tariff application by the US since the Smoot-Hawley tariffs which deepened the Great Depression and led to a collapse of world trade, which declined by 66% between 1929 and 1934.

The immediate situation is not alarming. But the tit-for-tat tariffs could get out of hand. The US is also involved in a tariff war with the European Union. In June, the EU put $3.2 billion tariff on US goods in retaliation for the Trump administration's steel and aluminum tariffs that came into effect on June 1, targeting products like bourbon, orange juice and motor cycles. India, which is also affected, says it will increase tariffs on 29 US products, including

"Global Economy Will Pay the Price of Escalating US-China Trade War," by Manoj Joshi, Observer Research Foundation, July 10, 2018. Reprinted by permission.

walnuts, chickpeas and almonds from August on. Canada and Mexico have slapped retaliatory tariffs on US exports as well.

Now, the US plans to hike tariffs on another $16 Billion worth of Chinese goods. After that, the sky is the limit. Trump has threatened that he could impose tariffs on all Chinese imports into the US totalling more than $500 billion. Beijing does not export that much to retaliate in kind, but respond it will.

The Fallout

According to analysts, the direct impact of the tariffs, even if 25% were to be imposed on everything the US imports from China, will only reduce Chinese growth by 0.5%. But the warfare could spread to other countries and to areas beyond trade. Already in June, the Trump administration had curbed visas for Chinese students and the administration and Congress are making plans to restrict Chinese investments and technology exports to China. As the ZTE instance revealed, this could be devastating for some of the Chinese giants.

However, the Chinese have sought to calm fears among US businesses that they would take recourse to unnecessary inspections, product quarantines, administrative punishments and regulatory delays to harass them. But there is no saying what direction the future could take. The "qualitative" measures that the Chinese threatened to take would not be easy to pin down.

Chinese vulnerabilities are manifest. These became evident when the US shut down ZTE in April, an act that brought the telecom giant to the brink of collapse because it cut off the supply of micro-chips needed for its products which are imported from the US. Essentially, while China may make phones, telecom equipment, computers which account for a third of its exports, it requires to import chips from abroad.

Aware of this vulnerability, Beijing is trying to develop a chip industry by hook or by crook. It has invested $150 billion to build the industry through its Made in China programmes. As a part of this, it has been seeking to buy established manufacturers abroad, as well as putting in a great deal of R&D effort at home.

The US is well positioned in its offensive. Its economy had grown at a brisk pace and the jobless rate has declined even further and wages and incomes are on the rise. So, for the present, the Trump administration does not have to worry too much. In this perspective, it could prove to be an electorally useful tool. This means that from the US point of view, it can stretch its fight to the coming year. On the other hand, China has been in the midst of trying to reduce the debt levels of its economy, leading to a slowdown of growth.

The rest of the world and India should not be particularly happy at the turn of events. A prolonged conflict and the disruption of global supply chains can have a ripple effect on the global economy. Many of the products facing American tariffs have components and assemblies that are made in third countries which would be affected as well. Indeed, given the way supply chains work, the US consumer could well end up paying higher costs for consumer products. An all-out trade war could lead to a collapse of global trade and shove the world economy towards a recession.

The Bigger Picture

There is no doubt that the two principals see the issues as going beyond just trade and tariffs.

A strong section of the Trump administration sees the struggle as one of primacy where China is seeking to craft a new industrial policy under the rubric of Made in China, to become the number one country in the area of artificial intelligence, robotics, aerospace applications, electrical vehicles and biotechnology. They have made no bones about their desire to promote their companies in these areas. The Made in China programme was outlined in a public document by China's Cabinet, the State Council. Equally, the Trump administration now says that China has all along been cheating the US by illegally acquiring technology worth hundreds of billions of dollars and tilting the playing field against foreign companies in China.

A larger struggle that has been unleashed ever since the US came up with its new National Security Strategy document that has depicted China, along with Russia, as strategic competitors. For decades, western countries believed that China would eventually become a market economy, but what China has been saying and doing is to make it clear that while the market is used to allocate some resources, the state led by the Communist Party of China runs the economy.

Despite everything, the Chinese still see this era as one of strategic opportunity. In his address to the important Central Conference on Work Relating to Foreign Affairs that was held in June, Xi noted that the world was "undergoing the most profound and unprecedented changes in a century" but that the period between now and the next Party Congress in 2022 was "a historical juncture for realising the two centenary goals of China."

Whether all this presages a new Cold War only the future will tell. But many specialists are arguing that this need not be seen in apocalyptic terms. Given the scale of their engagement and their global footprint, engagement between China and the US remains important for the world. There are many steps that can be taken before a total breakdown. The US could, for example, enhance its scrutiny of China's investments. Beijing, for its part needs to do much more to provide a level playing field for foreign investors. It has already signalled its desire to open up important sectors of its economy. However, China is unlikely to abandon its Made in China plans which can be slowed by the new US policy, but cannot be stopped.

To Understand the Benefits of Free Trade, Consider US History

Jason Margolis

Jason Margolis is a reporter with PRI's the World. *His work focuses on global business and economic issues as well as politics in the United States. Prior to his time at the* World, *he was a reporter for KQED Public Radio in Sacramento, the* Seattle Times, *and NPR.*

US President Donald Trump talks a lot about the evils of trade deals and trade imbalances. To combat this, one of his proposals is to slap tariffs—taxes on imports—on US trading partners.

Yet vast economic research shows: trade makes us much more prosperous. So, what's going on?

To understand how tariffs work, let's take a quick spin through the American history of trade and tariffs.

Let's say the year is 1750. If I lived in Massachusetts and you lived in New York, and I wanted to sell you a few things, we would've had some problems.

In those years, Britain's King George III restricted trade between the states; he wanted raw materials to flow through England first. Britain's mercantilist system wreaked havoc on the 13 Colonies.

"It ruined our banking system, which remained infantile until well after the [President Andrew] Jacksonian period," says economist Mike Hicks at Ball State University in Indiana.

"It prevented states from growing, I even think there's an argument to be made that it caused slavery to be more pervasive than it would've otherwise been because it prevented the manufacturing growth in Southern states that we would've seen," says Hicks.

King George wanted cotton from the South, not competition.

"The US Tried Extra-High Tariffs Before, in 1930. It Was a Disaster," by Jason Margolis, Public Radio International, February 1, 2017. Reprinted by permission.

But in 1776, the colonies declared independence. And the Founding Fathers wanted to make sure individual states didn't put up trade barriers against each other.

"Because they knew that would make everybody worse off," says Hicks. "The Interstate Commerce Clause in the Constitution was really designed to make the United States the world's first free trading bloc. And the prosperity that we have enjoyed for 241 years now really comes from that basic intuition."

But while the founders made interstate trade easy, they made international trade hard.

"We started as a high-tariff nation at the very beginning; it was Hamilton, Alexander Hamilton. You could say he kind of looked out the window one morning and said, 'What kind of economy is this?'" says Stephen S. Cohen, a professor emeritus with the University of California at Berkeley and author of the new book *Concrete Economics: The Hamilton Approach to Economic Growth and Policy*.

As the nation's first Treasury secretary, Hamilton pushed for a central bank, a strong federal government, and high tariffs to shelter infant industries.

"It was a general tariff, everything coming in, and it got up there 18, 20-some-odd percent, so this was a substantial protective barrier," says Cohen.

And that's basically how things went for the next century-and-a-half, with occasional exceptions.

Thanks, in part, to the tariff barrier, American manufacturers grew to become some of the world's most powerful companies. But American consumers had far less choice: If Americans needed, say, a chair in the 19th century, they either bought an American-made chair, or spent a lot of money on an exotic import.

Then came World War II and the United States emerged as the most powerful nation on Earth, and American leaders developed a new way of looking at commerce.

"Trade would help bring the nations together and help open up all these other economies and democratize them," says Cohen.

"And the central organizing question became very, very quickly after the war: Soviet communism."

More trade was seen as a bulwark against communist expansion. And, as young industries had matured, they also didn't need as much government protection from foreign competition.

And so, from the late 1940s until today, with infrequent exceptions on a few goods, US tariffs have remained basically close to zero. The results: Now we can buy less expensive chairs from across the globe, American exporters have new markets, and yes, many Americans have lost jobs to foreign competition.

But the vast majority of economists in the US agree: more free trade brings more overall prosperity.

For 12 presidential administrations, leaders from both parties followed this advice. Then, Trump burst onto the scene. He's threatened tariffs of 45 percent on China and 35 percent on Mexico, two of the United States' biggest trading partners.

It's not unprecedented. American leaders imposed dramatically high tariffs before with an infamous act of Congress passed in 1930, the Smoot-Hawley Tariff Act. In the late 1920s, more than a thousand economists warned American leaders against hiking tariffs on more than 20,000 imported goods to as much as 60 percent.

"But President Herbert Hoover, desperate to ensure his own re-election and wanting to curry favor with workers who were increasingly worried about an economic slowdown, signed the bill in 1930," says economist Lee Branstetter with Carnegie Mellon University in Pittsburgh. "History tells us what happened next. Soaring American tariffs set off a global trade war, our trading partners retaliated, and global trade fell sharply, deepening the Great Depression."

Many historians argue that the deteriorating world economy helped set the stage for World War II, a sobering thought.

So, if Trump imposes especially high tariffs, could it set off another global trade war?

"It's possible, it is very possible," says Cohen. "He said he's going to slap 45 percent tariffs on everything coming out of China. I don't know, let's say he does it. I would hate to be owning Apple Stock or Boeing stock that morning."

Meaning: China could quickly retaliate against American interests. And those iPhones made in China? A tariff would immediately make them even more expensive for American consumers.

But Trump has argued all along that if we curb imports from China we'll start building again in the United States. Problem is, it doesn't work like this. If China stops assembling iPhones, workers in lower-wage countries, like Vietnam or Malaysia, would likely pick up the slack, not people in Ohio and Indiana. And remember, that's Trump's stated goal in all of this: bringing jobs back home.

Some political analysts think Trump's talk of tariffs is just political bluster or perhaps an empty threat.

Cohen says, whatever the president is thinking, he has tapped into how large swaths of the country feel about trade.

"What we've had is some of us have benefitted from trade and some of us have lost badly," says Cohen.

Economists of all stripes have varied recommendations on how to create jobs in places like the Rust Belt. But it's hard to find any, from the right or the left—as well as business leaders or Republican leaders in Congress—who think imposing high tariffs is the right answer.

CHAPTER 2

Does Free Trade
Benefit Investors at the
Expense of Workers?

A History of Economic Theory on Trade Policy

William Krist

William Krist is a global fellow at the Woodrow Wilson International Center for Scholars. He is also a consultant and has provided analysis on a variety of topics related to international economics and politics.

Economists have had an enormous impact on trade policy, and they provide a strong rationale for free trade and for removal of trade barriers. Although the objective of a trade agreement is to liberalize trade, the actual provisions are heavily shaped by domestic and international political realities. The world has changed enormously from the time when David Ricardo proposed the law of comparative advantage, and in recent decades economists have modified their theories to account for trade in factors of production, such as capital and labor, the growth of supply chains that today dominate much of world trade, and the success of neomercantilist countries in achieving rapid growth.

Almost all Western economists today believe in the desirability of free trade, and this is the philosophy advocated by international institutions such as the World Bank, the International Monetary Fund, and the World Trade Organization (WTO). And this was the view after World War II, when Western leaders launched the General Agreement on Tariffs and Trade (GATT) in 1947.

However, economic theory has evolved substantially since the time of Adam Smith, and it has evolved rapidly since the GATT was founded. To understand US trade agreements and how they should proceed in the future, it is important to review economic theory and see how it has evolved and where it is today.

In the seventeenth and eighteenth centuries, the predominant thinking was that a successful nation should export more than it

"Trade Agreements and Economic Theory," by William Krist, Johns Hopkins University Press, 2013. Reprinted by permission.

imports and that the trade surplus should be used to expand the nation's treasure, primarily gold and silver. This would allow the country to have a bigger and more powerful army and navy and more colonies.

One of the better-known advocates of this philosophy, known as mercantilism, was Thomas Mun, a director of the British East India Company. In a letter written in the 1630s to his son, he said: "The ordinary means therefore to increase our wealth and treasure is by Foreign Trade, wherein wee must ever observe this rule; to sell more to strangers yearly than wee consume of theirs in value … By this order duly kept in our trading … that part of our stock which is not returned to us in wares must necessarily be brought home in treasure."[1]

Mercantilists believed that governments should promote exports and that governments should control economic activity and place restrictions on imports if needed to ensure an export surplus. Obviously, not all nations could have an export surplus, but mercantilists believed this was the goal and that successful nations would gain at the expense of those less successful. Ideally, a nation would export finished goods and import raw materials, under mercantilist theory, thereby maximizing domestic employment.

Then Adam Smith challenged this prevailing thinking in *The Wealth of Nations* published in 1776.[2] Smith argued that when one nation is more efficient than another country in producing a product, while the other nation is more efficient at producing another product, then both nations could benefit through trade. This would enable each nation to specialize in producing the product where it had an absolute advantage, and thereby increase total production over what it would be without trade. This insight implied very different policies than mercantilism. It implied less government involvement in the economy and a reduction of barriers to trade.

[…]

The Economic Effects of Trade Liberalization

The objective of reducing barriers to trade, of course, is to increase the level of trade, which is expected to improve economic well-being. Economists often measure economic well-being in terms of the share of total output of goods and services (i.e., gross domestic product, GDP) that the country produces per person on average. GDP is the best measurement of economic well-being available, but it has significant conceptual difficulties. As Joseph Stiglitz notes, the measurement of GDP fails "to capture some of the factors that make a difference in people's lives and contribute to their happiness, such as security, leisure, income distribution and a clean environment—including the kinds of factors which growth itself needs to be sustainable."[3] Moreover, GDP does not distinguish between "good growth" and "bad growth"; for example, if a company dumps waste in a river as a by-product of its manufacturing, both the manufacturing and the subsequent cleaning up of the river contribute to the measurement of GDP.

As the result of a multilateral round of trade negotiations under the GATT/WTO, tariffs are reduced during a transition period but are not completely eliminated. In the United States' bilateral or regional free trade agreements (FTAs), however, parties to the agreement completely eliminate almost all tariffs on trade with each other, generally over a transition period, which may be five to ten years.

Although reducing barriers to trade generally represents a move toward free trade, there are situations when reducing a tariff can actually increase the effective rate of protection for a domestic industry. Jacob Viner gives an example: "Let us suppose that there are import duties both on wool and on woolen cloth, but that no wool is produced at home despite the duty. Removing the duty on wool while leaving the duty unchanged on the woolen cloth results in increased protection for the cloth industry while having no significance for wool-raising."[4]

This happens for some products as a result of multilateral trade negotiations. For example, a country often reduces tariffs on products that are not import sensitive—often because they are not produced in that country—to a greater extent than it reduces tariffs on import sensitive products. In an FTA, where the end result is zero tariffs, this would not be an effect when the agreement is fully implemented. However, during the transition period it could well be relevant for some products. Other than this exception, however, reducing tariffs or other barriers to trade increases trade in the product, and this is the intent of the trade agreement.

The benefits to an economy from expanded exports as a trade partner improves market access are clear and indisputable. If the United States' trade partner reduces barriers as a result of a trade agreement, US exports will likely increase, which expands US production and GDP. And suppliers to a firm that gains additional sales through exports will likely also increase their sales to that firm, thereby increasing GDP further.

The firms gaining sales through this may well hire more workers and possibly increase dividends to stockholders. This money is distributed through the economy a number of times as a result of what economists call the money multiplier effect, which states that for every $1 an individual receives as income, a portion of it will be spent (i.e., consumption) and a portion will be saved. If individuals save 10 percent of their income, for every $1 earned as income, 90 cents will be spent and 10 cents will be saved. The 90 cents that is spent then becomes income for another individual, and once again 90 percent of this will be spent on consumption. This continues until there is nothing left from the original $1 amount.

[...]

This would suggest that the mercantilists were right, that a nation would be well advised to restrict imports. However, almost all economists today would reject that conclusion, and in fact many economists believe that reducing its trade barriers benefits a country whether or not the country's trade partners also reduce their barriers. Adam Smith and many economists after him argue that the objective of production is to produce goods for consumption. Stephen Cohen and his colleagues express this argument as follows: "The theories of comparative advantage (both classical and neoclassical) imply that liberalizing trade is always beneficial to consumers in any country, regardless of whether the country's trading partners reciprocate by reducing their own trade barriers. From this perspective, the emphasis on the reciprocal lowering of trade barriers in most actual trade liberalization efforts ... is misplaced."[5]

The benefits of unilateral elimination of trade barriers are particularly obvious in those cases where the country does not produce the product; in these cases, eliminating trade barriers expands consumer choice. (As noted above, however, an exception to this occurs in situations where reducing a trade barrier on a raw material or component that is not produced by the country increases the effective rate of protection for the finished product.)

Even where the country does produce the product, increased competition from trade liberalization will likely lead to lower prices by the domestic firms. In this event, some of the consumer's savings will then be spent consuming other products. The amount spent consuming other products will have positive production effects, which will somewhat mitigate the loss in production by the firm competing with the imports.

Increased import competition also has dynamic benefits by forcing domestic producers to become more efficient in order to compete in the lower price environment. Lower prices also may have a positive impact on monetary policy; because import competition reduces the threat of inflation, central banks can pursue a more liberal monetary policy of lower interest rates than otherwise would be the case. These lower rates benefit investment, housing, and other productive sectors.

[...]

Creating Comparative Advantages

The classic Western model of trade was based on eighteenth-century economic realities. Factors of production were relatively fixed: Land was immobile (although its fertility or usage might change), and labor mobility was highly restricted by political constraints. For most of the century, the movement of capital across borders was limited by political barriers and a lack of knowledge of other markets. (However, by the middle of the nineteenth century both capital and labor were flowing more freely between Europe and the Americas.) Technology in the eighteenth century was relatively simple by today's standards and was relatively similar in all countries. Additionally, the production of most products at that time was subject to diminishing returns, which meant that as production increased, the costs of producing each additional unit increased.

In this world, the classic Ricardian model of trade provided a good explanation for trade patterns, such as which countries would produce what products. England would produce textiles based on its wool production and capital availability, and Portugal would produce wine based on its sunshine and fertile soil. If Portugal chose to impose barriers to the importation of British textiles, its own economy would be less well off, and it would still be in Britain's interest to allow the free importation of Portuguese wine.

However, the world economy began to change in the twentieth century, as some products could be produced under conditions of increasing returns to scale. As a company produced more steel, production could be automated and the costs of each additional unit could be significantly reduced. And the same was true for automobiles and a growing number of other more sophisticated products.

By the last twenty-five years of the twentieth century, the global economy was significantly different. Land and labor were still relatively fixed, although capital could again move more freely around the world. However, technology was highly differentiated among countries, with the United States leading in many areas.

An established company in an industry that required extensive capital investment and knowledge had an enormous advantage over potential competitors. Its production runs were large, enabling it to produce product at low marginal cost. And the capital investment for a new competitor would be large.

In this new world, the economic policies pursued by a nation could create a new comparative advantage. A country could promote education and change its labor force from unskilled to semiskilled or even highly skilled. Or it could provide subsidies for research and development to create new technologies. Or it could take policy actions to force transfer of technology or capital from another country, such as allowing its companies to pirate technology from competitors or imposing a requirement that foreign investors transfer technology.

Ralph Gomory and William Baumol describe this well:

> The underlying reason for these significant departures from the original model is that the modern free-trade world is so different from the original historical setting of the free trade models. Today there is no one uniquely determined best economic outcome based on natural national advantages. Today's global economy does not single out a single best outcome, arrived at by international competition in which each country serves the world's best interests by producing just those goods that it can naturally turn out most efficiently. Rather, there are many possible outcomes that depend on what countries actually choose to do, what capabilities, natural or human-made, they actually develop.[6]

In the world of the late twentieth century, a country might be dominant in an industry because of its innate comparative advantage, or it might be dominant because of a strong boost from government policy, or it might be dominant because of historical accident. For example, the US dominance in aircraft was probably due to a strong educational system that produced highly competent engineers, a large domestic market with a dedicated customer (the U.S. military), and the historical accident that the aircraft industries of the United States' major competitors—Japan, Germany, and England—had all been destroyed in World War II.

Once such an industry becomes dominant, it is extremely difficult for other countries' industries to compete. The capital costs of entry may be very large, and it is difficult for a new entrant to master the technology. Additionally, the industry normally has a web of suppliers that are critical to competitiveness, such as steel companies and tire manufacturers. However, if such an industry losses its dominance, it is equally difficult for it to reenter the market.

A country with such a dominant industry benefits enormously economically. Because of its dominant position, such an industry may pay high wages and provide a stable base of employment.

Access to other markets plays an important role in this economic model where comparative advantage can be created. Without free trade, it becomes extremely costly for a government to subsidize a new entrant because the subsidy must be large enough both to overcome foreign trade barriers and to jump-start the domestic producer. The WTO and the United States' FTAs also play an important role by setting out rules that govern what actions a country may take in many areas to create comparative advantage; for example, the subsidies code limits the type of subsidies that governments may grant.

Gomory and Baumol note that because countries can create a comparative advantage in goods with decreasing costs of production, there are many possible outcomes to trade patterns: "These outcomes vary in their consequences for the economic well-being of the countries involved. Some of these outcomes are good for one country, some are good for the other, some are good for both. But it often is true that the outcomes that are the very best for one country tend to be poor outcomes for its trading partner."[7]

Although country policies can lead to creation of a dominant industry, such an industry may not be as efficient as if it had occurred in another country. An example given by Gomory and Baumol is Japan's steel industry. Japan has no domestic energy supplies and high wages; by contrast, China "has low labor costs and lots of coal."[8] In theory, China would be the efficient producer of steel, but in reality Japan is the dominant producer. (This example is less valid today, as China has become a major steel producer.)

Although there are many areas where government policies can create comparative advantage, there are still many areas where the classic assumptions of an inherent comparative advantage still hold. The key is whether the industry is subject to constant or increasing costs, such as wheat, or decreasing costs, such as autos, aircraft, or semiconductors.

[…]

Conclusion

Most economists today consider the law of comparative advantage to be one of the fundamental principles of economics. However, several very important caveats to the law of comparative advantage are often overlooked or glossed over.

First, David Ricardo based his theory on the assumption that the costs of production increase as production expands; in other words, each additional unit produced costs more than the previous unit, and this is true for many products, such as wheat. This assumption implies that countries have a comparative advantage in certain goods because of their natural endowment. However, many products today are produced under conditions of decreasing costs; for example, the cost of producing each additional semiconductor or airplane decreases as production expands. The extremely important implication of this is that countries can create comparative advantage.

A second extremely important caveat is the so-called factor price equalization theorem, which holds that international trade will cause the relative returns to factors of production, such as unskilled labor, to equalize between countries under free trade conditions. This would mean that for a high-wage country such as the United States, wages for unskilled workers would fall while wages in labor abundant countries would rise. However, factor prices will not tend to equalize in industries that have decreasing costs of production.

Third, Ricardo and other early economists based their theories on trade in goods, and they did not consider trade in factors of production. Today, however, basic factors of production such as labor, capital, and technology are traded. The implication of trade in factors of production is that factor equalization will occur completely in a shorter time period than would occur under trade in goods only.

Fourth, Western economic theory assumes that trade will be reasonably balanced over time. Where this is not the case, it indicates that the deficit country will be importing products where it would normally have a comparative advantage; if these products are in areas that experience decreasing costs of production, over time the industry may lose its ability to compete in global markets.

The world has changed since the time of Smith and Ricardo. Today, trade is no longer mostly between small producers and farmers but giant global corporations that buy parts and materials from around the world and sell globally. These giant supply chains were made possible by trade liberalization and technology changes, and they account for the fact that international trade has expanded far more rapidly than global economic growth since 1970. These global supply chains also have implications for strategies for developing countries in promoting economic growth.

Clearly, the United States benefits when its trade partners reduce their trade barriers, because its exports will increase, which generates expanded production and employment. Most economists also believe that the United States benefits from reducing its own trade barriers, as consumers gain from reduced costs and producers are forced by international competition to improve efficiency. However, import liberalization has an impact on domestic labor and production that needs to be considered.

Multilateral trade liberalization, where all countries reduce their trade barriers in parallel, best promotes trade based on comparative advantage. However, countries can abuse the system by adopting beggar-thy-neighbor policies.

Notes

1. Thomas Mun, in a letter written to his son in the 1630s, available at http://socserv .mcmaster.ca/econ/ugcm/3ll3/mun/treasure.txt.

2. William Bernstein notes that [Adam] Smith was not the first to advocate the advantages of free trade. He says, "By far the most remarkable early free-trader was Henry Martyn, whose *Considerations upon the East India Trade* preceded by seventy-five years Adam Smith's *Wealth of Nations*." William J. Bernstein, *A Splendid Exchange: How Trade Shaped the World* (New York: Grove Press, 2008), 258.

3. Stiglitz, *Progress, What Progress*, 27.

4. Jacob Viner, *The Customs Union Issue* (New York: Carnegie Endowment for International Peace, 1950), 48.

5. Stephen D. Cohen, Robert A. Blecker, and Peter D. Whitney, *Fundamentals of US Foreign Trade Policy: Economics, Politics, Laws, and Issues* (Boulder, Colo.: Westview Press, 2003), 57.

6. Ralph Gomory and William Baumol, *Global Trade and Conflicting National Interests* (Cambridge, Mass.: MIT Press, 2000), 5.

7. Ibid., 5.

8. Ibid., 21.

The Impact of Globalization on Labor Markets and Income Distribution

Uri Dadush and William Shaw

Uri Dadush is a senior fellow at the OCP Policy Center in Rabat, Morocco, and a consultant with Economic Policy International LLC. William Shaw is a former visiting scholar in the Carnegie Endowment's International Economics Program and a former staff member of the World Bank's research department.

The blame for three decades of stagnant wages in most advanced countries is often laid at the doorstep of globalization, particularly competition from low-wage developing exporters. Globalization is clearly contributing to increased integration of labor markets and closing the wage gap between workers in advanced and developing economies, especially through the spread of technology. It also plays a part in increasing domestic income inequality. But erecting protectionist policies to stanch the forces of globalization is not the best response. Policymakers must instead focus on what can be done to help workers adjust to a changing world.

The Imperfect Integration of Labor Markets

We are very far from a global labor market, as evidenced by a wide disparity in wages. One study finds that the median wage for jobs in advanced countries is two and a half times the wage level for jobs with similar skill levels in the most advanced developing countries, and five times the level in low-income countries. In 2008, a Chinese manufacturing worker earned about one-twentieth the wage level of a US manufacturing worker; a Mexican, one-sixth.

That gap, however, is narrowing in part due to globalization. From 1999 to 2009 (the year of the worst global recession since the 1930s), average real wages rose by about 0.5 percent per year

"Globalization, Labor Markets, and Inequality," by Uri Dadush and William Shaw, Carnegie Endowment for International Peace, February 2, 2012. Reprinted by permission.

in advanced countries, compared to about 1.5 percent in Africa and Latin America, and almost 8 percent in developing Asia.

Globalization is far from being the whole story behind the narrowing gaps. If wage convergence were principally the result of an integrating global labor market, one would see wages in Africa, the poorest region, rise much faster than the others. But differences in domestic factors, such as the business climate, governance, and education, also play a vital role in determining wage growth.

Global Forces Behind Wage Convergence

Migration, trade, foreign investment, and the spread of technology—all channels of globalization—work to induce wage convergence in interconnected and mutually reinforcing ways.

Increased migration probably plays only a small role in wage convergence. The stock of emigrants from developing countries is just 2 percent of their population, so emigration has little role in raising wages by limiting the growth in labor supply in developing countries. Most studies have found that immigration also has had only modest long-term effects on wages in advanced countries. There are many potential reasons for this: Immigrants typically only account for 10–15 percent of the labor force. Migrants and native workers are imperfect substitutes and may even complement each other, as migrants increase aggregate demand for the services of native workers. And migrants reduce the price of services consumed by native workers.

Trade can promote wage convergence even when workers do not move. Developing countries with abundant labor export goods intensive in labor, so trade induces their wages to rise relative to rich countries, which have less labor and plenty of capital. The more-than-quadrupling of developing countries' manufactures exports relative to their GDP from 1985 to 2008 almost certainly contributed to wage convergence, especially in middle-income countries that have typically been the most successful exporters. Numerous studies of the direct impact of trade on wages in advanced countries conclude that the depressing effect is small.

Foreign direct investment (FDI) in capital-scarce developing countries can raise the productivity of workers, and thus their wages, by transferring management skills, capital, and technology, and in the process sometimes outsourcing jobs from advanced countries. FDI inflows to developing countries rose from 0.6 percent of their GDP in 1980 to 3.5 percent in 2008. However, over the past decade, total net capital flows (including official and private portfolio flows) equal to 2.6 percent of developing countries' GDP actually have gone from developing to advanced countries, largely in the form of Treasury bill purchases. This type of investment did not generate jobs directly in advanced countries, but may have reduced the need for domestic borrowing that would have crowded out domestic investors. On balance, it is therefore not clear whether capital flows to and from developing countries have played a large role in promoting wage convergence, though capital flows taking the form of FDI almost certainly have.

Various studies have shown that skill-biased technological change is a major driver in reducing the demand for unskilled workers. At the same time, the transfer of all types of technology through FDI, international trade (imports of machines and learning from competitors and sophisticated customers), and migration (via contacts with diasporas and returning migrants) from advanced to developing countries provides an enormously important opportunity for raising productivity and thus wages in the latter. Moreover, increased competition from low-wage countries tends to spur labor-saving technology in advanced countries.

However, despite the deepening of these channels, remaining barriers to trade and investment, inefficiencies in transport and communications, and structural limitations to the absorption of technology in developing countries, such as insufficient levels of education and business climates that discourage ventures that could adopt technologies, continue to impede the spread of technology. Moreover, in many poor countries, even relatively old technologies are only available in selected locales and to elites, or used only by a few firms. Thus much of the technology adoption that contributes to wage convergence is actually about bringing backward regions, inefficient firms, and disadvantaged groups up to the level of the more advanced in the same country.

Globalization of the Labor Market and Income Distribution

These forces of globalization have been associated with both rising living standards and a deterioration in income distribution in advanced countries: Low-skilled wages have remained flat or even declined, while high-skilled wages have increased sharply. Labor income fell as a share of GDP by 3.5 percentage points from 1993 to 2009. And Gini coefficients, which provide an aggregate measure of income inequality, rose from the mid-1980s to the mid-2000s in all G-7 countries except France.

Inequality also has increased in many developing countries. According to the International Labor Organization, of the 28 developing countries for which data are available, 21 experienced increased income inequality from the early 1990s to the mid-2000s. As in advanced countries, openness to trade and foreign investment have increased the relative return to skilled labor and capital, while reducing the relative return to unskilled labor.

Indeed, some analyses find that trade and financial liberalization episodes, or openness in general, have contributed to worsening income inequality, at least in the middle-income countries. The link between openness and inequality depends in part on the policies adopted, as well as the structure of the economy and the initial income distribution.

How Should Policymakers Respond?

Developing countries' weak social safety nets and relatively unequal income distributions make them very sensitive to the impact on the losers from globalization. However, their rapid growth and good fiscal positions mean that over time they should be able to build the safety nets available to workers in advanced countries. In designing safety nets, policymakers in developing countries should try to protect workers if unemployed or injured, but would be ill-advised to erect the barriers to firing common in many advanced countries that reduce the overall demand for labor in formal (that is, decent) employment.

Despite their wealth, the labor challenge facing advanced countries, still mired in high unemployment in the wake of the crisis, is more daunting. Identifying the correct policy response is made more arduous by the difficulty of attributing the worsening of income distribution with any precision to trade, technology, demography (increased female participation in the labor force, for example), or other factors such as increasing returns to education.

What is certain is that the answer cannot be to stop the spread of technology or trade. With developing countries likely to be home to the vast majority of the global middle class—people with significant disposable income—in the coming decades, the opportunities available to advanced countries from international trade and technological innovation are likely to greatly increase. At the same time, competition in technology-intensive sectors as developing countries learn will intensify, forcing the pace of innovation to increase even more.

The US tax code could be made more progressive by increasing rates for the highest-income taxpayers, eliminating deductions that favor higher-income groups, reducing social security taxes that weigh most heavily on wage earners, and eliminating unproductive tax loopholes that favor corporations.

But taxes are only part of the problem. Poverty has also been driven by an erosion of the quality of public goods. Most importantly, public education in many advanced countries, beginning with the United States, no longer offers the same opportunities for advancement that it did in the first half of the twentieth century. Increased investment in education and training is all the more important with rapid technological progress and shifts in the demand for workers with different skill levels.

Globalized markets may be changing too quickly to provide the security enjoyed by manufacturing workers in the 1950s. Setting up trade barriers in an attempt to slow the pace of change is not an appropriate response, as they would in effect throw out the baby (efficiency) with the bathwater (inequality). But a much better job can be done to soften the blow for those who are adversely affected and help workers adjust to the demands of a rapidly changing global economy.

Why International Cooperation on Labor Standards Is Important

International Labour Organization

The International Labour Organization (ILO) is an agency within the United Nations that establishes international labor standards and works to promote opportunities for workers around the world.

The challenges of globalization have made international labour standards more relevant than ever. What benefits do they provide today?

A Path to Decent Work

International labour standards are first and foremost about the development of people as human beings. In the ILO's Declaration of Philadelphia of 1944, the international community recognized that "labour is not a commodity". Indeed, labour is not like an apple or a television set, an inanimate product that can be negotiated for the highest profit or the lowest price. Work is part of everyone's daily life and is crucial to a person's dignity, well-being and development as a human being. Economic development should include the creation of jobs and working conditions in which people can work in freedom, safety and dignity. In short, economic development is not undertaken for its own sake but to improve the lives of human beings; international labour standards are there to ensure that it remains focused on improving human life and dignity.

An International Framework for Fair and Stable Globalization

Achieving the goal of decent work in the globalized economy requires action at the international level. The world community is responding to this challenge in part by developing international

"The Benefits of International Labour Standards," International Labour Organization, 2018. Reprinted by permission. © 2018 ILO.

legal instruments on trade, finance, environment, human rights and labour. The ILO contributes to this legal framework by elaborating and promoting international labour standards aimed at making sure that economic growth and development go along with the creation of decent work. The ILO's unique tripartite structure ensures that these standards are backed by governments, employers, and workers alike. International labour standards therefore lay down the basic minimum social standards agreed upon by all players in the global economy.

A Level Playing Field

An international legal framework on social standards ensures a level playing field in the global economy. It helps governments and employers to avoid the temptation of lowering labour standards in the belief that this could give them a greater comparative advantage in international trade. In the long run such practices do not benefit anyone. Lowering labour standards can encourage the spread of low-wage, low-skill, and high-turnover industries and prevent a country from developing more stable high-skilled employment, while at the same time making it more difficult for trading partners to develop their economies upwards. Because international labour standards are minimum standards adopted by governments and the social partners, it is in everyone's interest to see these rules applied across the board, so that those who do not put them into practice do not undermine the efforts of those who do.

A Means of Improving Economic Performance

International labour standards are sometimes perceived as entailing significant costs and thus hindering economic development. A growing body of research indicates, however, that compliance with international labour standards often accompanies improvements in productivity and economic performance. Higher wage and working time standards and respect for equality can translate into better and more satisfied workers and lower turnover of staff.

Investment in vocational training can result in a better-trained workforce and higher employment levels.[1] Safety standards can reduce costly accidents and health care fees. Employment protection can encourage workers to take risks and to innovate. Social protection such as unemployment schemes and active labour market policies can facilitate labour market flexibility; they make economic liberalization and privatization sustainable and more acceptable to the public. Freedom of association and collective bargaining can lead to better labour-management consultation and cooperation, thereby reducing the number of costly labour conflicts and enhancing social stability.

The beneficial effects of labour standards do not go unnoticed by foreign investors. Studies have shown that in their criteria for choosing countries in which to invest, foreign investors rank workforce quality and political and social stability above low labour costs. At the same time, there is little evidence that countries which do not respect labour standards are more competitive in the global economy.[2]

A Safety Net in Times of Economic Crisis

Even fast-growing economies with high-skilled workers can experience unforeseen economic downturns. The Asian financial crisis of 1997, the 2000 Dot-Com Bubble burst and the 2008 financial and economic crisis showed how decades of economic growth could be undone by dramatic currency devaluations or falling market prices. For instance, during the 1997 Asian crisis, as well as the 2008 crisis, unemployment increased significantly in many of the countries affected. The disastrous effects of these crises on workers were compounded by the fact that in many of these countries social protection systems (notably unemployment and health insurance), active labour market policies and social dialogue were non-existent or under tremendous pressure. Taking an approach that balances macroeconomic and employment goals, while at the same time taking social impacts into account, can help to address these challenges.[3]

A Strategy for Reducing Poverty

Economic development has always depended on the acceptance of rules. Legislation and functioning legal institutions ensure property rights, the enforcement of contracts, respect for procedure, and protection from crime—all legal elements of good governance without which no economy can operate. A market governed by a fair set of rules and institutions is more efficient and brings benefit to everyone. The labour market is no different. Fair labour practices set out in international labour standards and applied through a national legal system ensure an efficient and stable labour market for workers and employers alike.

In many developing and transition economies, a large part of the work-force is active in the informal economy. Moreover, such countries often lack the capacity to provide effective social justice. Yet international labour standards can be effective tools in these situations as well. Most standards apply to all workers, not just those working under formal work arrangements; some standards, such as those dealing with homeworkers, migrant and rural workers, and indigenous and tribal peoples, actually deal specifically with areas of the informal economy. The extension of freedom of association, social protection, occupational safety and health, vocational training, and other measures required by international labour standards have proved to be effective strategies in reducing poverty and bringing workers into the formal economy. Furthermore, international labour standards call for the creation of institutions and mechanisms which can enforce labour rights. In combination with a set of defined rights and rules, functioning legal institutions can help formalize the economy and create a climate of trust and order which is essential for economic growth and development.[4]

The Sum of International Experience and Knowledge

International labour standards are the result of discussions among governments, employers and workers, in consultation with experts from around the world. They represent the international consensus on how a particular labour problem could be tackled at the global level and reflect knowledge and experience from all corners of the world. Governments, employers' and workers' organizations, international institutions, multinational companies and non-governmental organizations can benefit from this knowledge by incorporating the standards in their policies, operational objectives and day-to-day action. The standards' legal character allows them to be used in the legal system and administration at the national level, and as part of the corpus of international law which can bring about greater integration of the international community.

Notes

1. OECD, "OECD Skills Outlook 2013," *First Results from the Survey of Adult Skills*, OECD, Paris, 2013.

2. D. Kucera, "Core Labour Standards and Foreign Direct Investment," *International Labour Review*, vol. 141, no. 1–2 (2002), pp. 31–70.

3. "World of Work Report 2013," *Repairing the Economic and Social Fabric*, International Institute for Labour Studies, ILO, Geneva, 2013.

4. ILO, *Transitioning from the Informal to the Formal Economy*, vol. 1, International Labour Conference, 103rd Session, Geneva, 2014.

Globalization and the Distribution of Its Benefits

Xavier Devictor

Xavier Devictor is an economist currently serving as advisor to the Fragility, Conflict, and Violence Group at the World Bank. He has also worked on public sector management programs in Europe and Africa.

I s globalization a good or a bad thing? Does it benefit everybody or mainly the "banksters"? There have been many debates about globalization and inequalities, but what is the evidence?

Global inequalities started to rise with the Industrial Revolution, when a score of countries experienced much faster economic growth than the rest of the world. This gave them an advantage which they kept until the beginning of the globalization era. A "catching up" phenomenon is now at play, with some of the poorest countries having emerged and turned into global engines of growth. It is too early to pass a definitive judgment, but it seems that inequality across countries has started to decline since the late 1990s. On the other hand, there is evidence that in some countries globalization has been accompanied by an increase of inequalities—as recently raised by people as different as Pope Francis and President Obama.

Yet, in a recent paper, a World Bank researcher, Branko Milanovic, looked at the question from a different perspective—what if we forget for a moment about borders and measure inequality among individuals (not nations)? What if we do not compare, say, Poland to Germany, or rich and poor in Poland, but each person in the world to all others? Would we see global inequalities, those between the world's richest and poorest citizens regardless of where they live, on the rise or in decline ? The study provides

"Is Globalization a Good or a Bad Thing?" by Xavier Devictor, The World Bank Group, February 11, 2014. Reprinted by permission.

some interesting insights on the nature of inequality in the age of globalization.

As could be expected, it shows that the world remains a tremendously unequal place. Using a standard indicator (the Gini coefficient), global inequality is far greater than inequality within any country, even the most unequal ones. The gap between a poor person in India or Sub-Saharan Africa and the Western upper-class is an abyss.

The study also shows that the determinant factor of one's income is where one lives. The poorest five percent of Germans are richer than the wealthiest five percent of Ivoirians. In other words, social classes matter less than places of residence (bye-bye Marx!). The consequences are clear—either poor countries can develop their economies fast, or their people will be inclined to migrate to richer shores.

Maybe most interestingly, the study looks at the winners and losers of the globalization process—and unveils several unexpected facts.

It is often assumed that there are two main groups who benefit from globalization—the "top 1 percent" and the "emerging middle class" in countries like China, India, etc. The numbers confirm these intuitions. But they also show that the income of the "emerging middle class" rose even faster than that of the top 1 percent. And that this "emerging middle class" accounts for about half of humankind. This is no small feat!

The study also shows that the people at the "global bottom" too have gained over the last decades, less than the "emerging middle class" but enough to reduce abject poverty dramatically (the exception is the poorest five percent of the world population, people who typically live in conflict-affected countries, and who have seen little benefits of a globalization process that has largely bypassed them). This is very encouraging.

In fact, the biggest losers of the globalization process may well be the "global upper middle class" (technically: those between the 75th and 90th percentile of income distribution), i.e., the poorest part of the population in Western European countries, the lower middle class in Central Europe. These groups have not lost out, but they have not seen their income rise in any meaningful manner over the last two decades while the rest of the world surged.

So what does it all mean for a country like Poland? In spite of common perceptions, Poland as a whole is already among the wealthiest countries in the world, even though of course not everybody in Poland is wealthy. The study highlights the need to accelerate economic growth, so as to increase as rapidly as possible the distance from the potentially swampy grounds of the "global upper middle class." It also suggests that continued policy action is needed to ensure that prosperity can be truly shared by all, that the gains of globalization are not captured by a "happy few," but on the contrary that all can take advantage of the opportunities offered by the globalization process, including those who earn the least. It highlights the importance of contributing to other countries' development to reduce the global inequalities which can be the seeds of geopolitical turmoil. And most importantly it provides a confirmation (with numbers!) that the world is indeed becoming a better place.

Everyone Benefits from a Global Free Trade Environment

Denise Froning

Denise Froning is a senior research analyst at the Charles Koch Institute and a former trade policy analyst at the Heritage Foundation's Center for International Trade and Economics. She is among the authors of the Heritage Foundation's Index of Economic Freedom.

The benefits of free trade are many and far outweigh any risks that foreign competition might pose to the US economy. These benefits fall into four major categories.

Benefit #1: Free Trade Promotes Innovation and Competition

Few people in America today sew all their own clothes, grow all their own food, build their own houses, or buy only products made in their own states. It would cost too much and take too much time, especially since Americans can acquire such items on the open market with relative ease. The same principle of practicality and cost applies on an international scale. It makes economic sense to buy a product from another who specializes in such production or who can make it more easily or for less cost.

Indeed, access to a greater variety of goods and services is the purpose of trade. Imports, then, are not a sacrifice, a necessary evil for the good of exporting. One exports so that one may acquire goods and services in return. This logic is evident on a personal level as well: A person works so that he has the means to buy necessities and possibly even luxuries. One does not make purchases in order to justify working.

"The Benefits of Free Trade: A Guide For Policymakers," by Denise Froning, The Heritage Foundation, August 25, 2000. Reprinted by permission.

Free trade is the only type of truly fair trade because it offers consumers the most choices and the best opportunities to improve their standard of living. It fosters competition, spurring companies to innovate and develop better products and to bring more of their goods and services to market, keeping prices low and quality high in order to retain or increase their market share.

Free trade also spurs innovation. The US market has demonstrated repeatedly, particularly over the last decade, that competition leads to increasing innovation. This is evident, for example, in the intense competition to create the latest personal computer at the lowest cost. With the growth of electronic commerce has come unlimited choices of goods and services and lower prices for products. Computers are now available for free just for signing an annual Internet provider service agreement.

In fact, America's greatest advantage lies in its ability to innovate and to build upon that continually expanding knowledge base. According to *The Economist*, the United States "has an 'innovational complex'—those thousands of entrepreneurs, venture capitalists, and engineers—unmatched anywhere in the world." This resource results in an ever-growing number of new products and services that bolster America's competitive advantage in the global market and greater prosperity at home.

This competitive advantage derives largely from America's open market practices. Free trade promotes innovation because, along with goods and services, the flow of trade circulates new ideas. Since companies must compete with their overseas counterparts, American firms can take note of all the successes as well as the failures that take place in the global marketplace. Consumers then benefit because companies in a freely competing market must either keep up with the leader in order to retain customers or innovate to create their own niche.

[...]

Benefit #2: Free Trade Generates Economic Growth

By fostering opportunities for American businesses, free trade rewards risk-taking by increasing sales, profit margins, and market share. Companies can choose to build on those profits by expanding their operations, entering new market sectors, and creating better-paying jobs. According to US Trade Representative [Charlene] Barshefsky, US exports support over 12 million jobs in America, and trade-related jobs pay an average of 13 percent to 16 percent higher wages than do non-trade-related jobs.

[…]

The growth in the US economy also benefits people in poor countries who have access to the US market, where both the demand for goods and services and levels of remuneration are much higher than they would be at home. To trade at this level enables their nascent businesses to acquire capital, fueling production and fostering the development of new industries. Impoverished people gain the opportunity to earn better wages, acquire more goods, and raise their standard of living.

In other words, this is a win-win scenario for Americans and people of countries that have been mired in poverty despite years of foreign aid. The advantage for poor countries in being able to trade for capital—rather than having to rely on ineffective assistance programs that are subject to waste or fraud—is that the payoff is more immediate in their private sectors. Foreign investment allows their domestic industries to develop and provide better employment opportunities for local workers. This dynamic makes an increase in foreign direct investment one of the most important benefits of free trade for developing nations.

Benefit #3: Free Trade Disseminates Democratic Values

Free trade fosters support for the rule of law. Companies that engage in international trade have reason to abide by the terms of their contracts and international agreed-upon norms and laws. The World Trade Organization, for example, compels its member countries to honor trade agreements and, in any trade dispute, to abide by the decisions of the WTO's mediating body.

By supporting the rule of law, free trade also can reduce the opportunities for corruption. In countries where contracts are not enforced, business relationships fail, foreign investors flee, and capital stays away. It is a downward spiral that especially hinders economic development in countries where official corruption is widespread. As Alejandro Chafuen, President of the Atlas Economic Research Foundation, has noted, "True economic freedom is possible only under a system of limited government with a strong rule of law. Economic freedom has little value if corruption in government means that only a few will enjoy it."

Trade likewise can falter quickly in countries where customs officials expect kickbacks at every checkpoint. In Western Africa, customs officials can stop trucks carrying goods as often as every hundred yards just to collect another bribe, as Mabousso Thiam, executive secretary of the West African Enterprise Network, testified at a 1999 Organisation for Economic Co-Operation and Development (OECD) conference on corruption. Such arbitrary checkpoints spring up when countries cannot pay their customs officials livable wages, forcing them to choose between remaining honest but failing to bring home enough money to feed their families or taking an illegal bribe, as others often do. As UN Secretary General Kofi Annan has observed,

> Corruption is built on everything being in the hands of the government. So for everything you want, you need a permit. The person who gives you the permit wants a bribe. The person who's going to make the appointment for you wants a bribe. And so on.

Free trade, reinforced by the rule of law, removes such incentives for corruption by spurring economic growth, increasing the number of better-paying jobs, and ultimately increasing the level of prosperity.

But free trade transmits more than just physical goods or services to people. It also transmits ideas and values. A culture of freedom can flourish whenever a great society, as 18th century economist Adam Smith termed it, emerges with the self-confidence to open itself to an inflow of goods and the ideas and practices accompanying them. A culture of freedom can become both the cornerstone and capstone of economic prosperity.

Benefit #4: Free Trade Fosters Economic Freedom

As the foregoing discussion shows, the ability to trade freely increases opportunity, choices, and standards of living. Countries with the freest economies today generally have adopted a capitalist model of economic development, remaining open to international trade and investment. These countries include the United Kingdom and many of its former colonies and dominions: Hong Kong, Singapore, New Zealand, the United States, Australia, and Canada.

Chile, which benefits from a diverse European heritage, likewise demonstrates that basing economic policies on a capitalist free-market model brings good results in that region as well.

Heritage's analysis of the 161 countries covered in the *Index of Economic Freedom*, published annually with *The Wall Street Journal*, indicates that free trade policies can foster development and raise the level of economic freedom. Every day in the marketplaces of free countries, individuals make choices and exercise direct control over their own lives. As economic growth occurs, note World Bank economists David Dollar and Aart Kraay, the poorest people can benefit just as much as—and in some cases more than—the wealthy. With a sound infrastructure based on economic freedom, assured property rights, a fair and independent judiciary, the free flow of capital, and a fair system of low taxation, poor countries can create an environment that is friendly to trade and inviting to foreign investors.

Consider the experience of China and Taiwan. In 1960, real per capita income in the People's Republic of China tracked closely with that of the Republic of China on Taiwan. In the late 1960s, however, the government in Taipei chose to institute widespread reforms to guarantee private property, establish a legal system to protect property rights and enforce contracts, reform the banking and financial systems, stabilize taxes, distribute public land to individuals, and allow the market to flourish. The result for Taiwan has been an astounding record of economic growth.

The *2000 Index of Economic Freedom* ranks Taiwan as the 11th freest economy in the world. With its economic freedom came the rise of democratic institutions. For the first time since the ruling party (the Kuomintang, or KMT) established a government in Taipei 50 years ago, a democratic transition of power took place in Taiwan as Chen Shui-bian, a candidate from a previously outlawed opposition party, assumed the presidency on May 20, 2000.

Despite this success, opponents of permanent normal trade relations with China argue that trade and economic liberalization will not bring democracy to mainland China or improve its human rights record. These critics assert that democracy is simply too foreign to the mainland—an argument that ironically echoes the mutterings of Asian authoritarian regimes about "Asian values." The development of political and economic freedom in Taiwan refutes such claims and points to the potential that more political and economic freedom can develop in China. Such an outcome would be in America's best interest because it would enhance regional stability, increase prosperity for the Chinese, and open China's immense market to Americans.

The US trade agreement with China signed by the Clinton Administration in November 1999 is a step in the right direction. It will help open the Chinese market to American exports and foreign direct investment to an unprecedented degree. Economic freedom is the biggest benefit of trade extension, both for American companies looking to invest in China and for the Chinese people themselves. These foundations of economic freedom not only will allow the Chinese people to gain access to the outside world, but also will expose the Chinese government to—and compel it to enforce—the international consensus on the rule of law. Such issues as property rights and honoring contracts, which companies historically have found to be a problem when trying to make deals in China, will be subject to a higher force.

Establishing the backbone of property rights and free-market policies is essential for creating the sort of market stability that is important to foreign investors. In countries with an established rule of law that does not ebb and flow from one leader to the next, foreign investors are more confident and willing to take risks in bringing businesses into developing nations. It is one reason Taiwan and Hong Kong, for example, have flourished over the past few decades.

[...]

Conclusion

Societies that enact free trade policies create their own economic dynamism—fostering a wellspring of freedom, opportunity, and prosperity that benefits every citizen. In recent years, the United States has demonstrated the power of this principle. Nor are American citizens alone in benefiting from those free trade policies that the US enacts. By breaking the cycle of poverty, America's free trade policies can enable even the most impoverished countries to begin to create their own dynamic toward prosperity.

Nevertheless, despite all the evidence to the contrary, the opponents of free trade will continue to espouse the old argument that "the jobs created by globalization are often less sustaining and secure than the livelihoods abolished by it [in poor countries]." Such a claim presupposes that some sort of agrarian utopia previously existed in these countries and that their peoples will not reap the benefits of economic development.

Clamoring to stop this wave of economic progress carried forward by technology and innovation is akin to arguing that the United States, to cite just one example, was better off before the Industrial Revolution. While one might argue that this was true of the white male members of the landed classes (although even then such a claim is dubious), for the majority of the population that did not enjoy such luxury, quality of life has improved immeasurably.

The Industrial Revolution brought freedom of movement and increased opportunity to all economic levels of society. It also set the stage for social and democratic progress of a magnitude that would have been impossible earlier. And although history suggests that this new era of market globalization may well be accompanied by new problems for which the solutions once again will lie in the power of human ingenuity and innovation, it also presents an unprecedented level of opportunity for people to achieve economic freedom and greater prosperity.

Evidence Shows that International Trade Agreements Benefit the US Labor Market

Brandon Scudder

Brandon Scudder is a writer for the National Customs Brokers & Forwarders Association of America, Inc. (NCBFAA). His work focuses on international trade.

International trade is the framework upon which American prosperity rests. Free trade policies have created a level of competition in today's open market that provokes continual innovation and leads to better products, better-paying jobs, new markets, and increased savings and investment. Free trade enables more goods and services to reach American consumers at lower prices, thereby substantially increasing their standard of living.

Free trade is an important component of our system of economic liberty. Under a system of natural liberty in which domestic commerce is largely free from restraints on competition, though not necessarily free from government regulation, commerce would also be permitted to operate freely between countries. Adam Smith, the author of *The Wealth of Nations in* 1776, made a case for free trade with a persuasiveness that is still visible to this day. Adam Smith advocated the system of natural liberty, one, that would allow individuals the right to pursue their own interests, while the government would provide the foundation or framework in which commerce would take place. President Reagan stated that, "government can and must provide opportunity, not smother it; foster productivity, not stifle it."

Free trade is the only type of truly fair trade because it offers consumers the most choices and the best opportunities to improve their standard of living. It promotes competition, spurring

"Do Free Trade Agreements Encourage Economic Development in the U.S.?" by Brandon Scudder, NCBFAA 2011 scholarship winner, National Customs Brokers & Forwarders Association of America, Inc., 2017. Reprinted by permission.

companies to innovate and develop better products and to bring more of their goods and services to market, keeping prices low and quality high in order to retain or increase their market share. For example, from 1990–1999, the US economy grew by more than 23 percent, adding more than $2.1 trillion to the nation's gross domestic product (GDP) and raising the wealth of the average American consumer by more than $5,500. The economy responded well to the expansion of trade that occurred after the signing of the North American Free Trade Agreement (NAFTA) in 1993 and the establishment of the World Trade Organization (WTO) in 1995 as an opportunity for settling trade disputes. The economy responded well and as a result the imports of real goods and services increased 115 percent, which, in turn increased the number of full-time jobs by 13.4 percent.

Free trade also spurs innovation. The US market has demonstrated repeatedly, particularly over the last decade that competition leads to increasing innovation. This is evident, for example, in the intense competition to create the newest and updated personal computer at the lowest cost. With the growth of electronic commerce have come unlimited choices of goods and services and lower prices for products. This competitive advantage derives largely from America's open market practices. Free trade promotes innovation because, along with goods and services, the flow of trade circulates new ideas. Since companies must compete with their overseas counterparts, American firms can take note of all the successes as well as the failures that take place in the global marketplace.

Consumers then benefit because companies in a freely competing market must either keep up with the leader in order to retain customers or innovate to create their own niche. Clearly, removing counterproductive barriers to competition, such as quotas and tariffs that limit access and competition is both good economic and public policy. Free trade, reinforced by the rule of law, removes such incentives for corruption by spurring economic growth, increasing the number of better-paying jobs, and ultimately increasing the level of prosperity.

By fostering opportunities for American businesses, free trade rewards risk-taking by increasing sales, profit margins, and market share. Companies can choose to build on those profits by expanding their operations, entering new market sectors, and creating better-paying jobs. This also allows American companies to saturate the market in a country that previously was without the goods and services a particular business offers. Consequently, if a trade market is not taken seriously, the market share for a good or service will be lost to its competition. According to US Trade Representative [Charlene] Barshefsky, US exports support over 12 million jobs in America, and trade-related jobs pay an average of 13 percent to 16 percent higher wages than do non-trade related jobs.

The nature of employment in the United States is indeed evolving away from manufacturing and toward more service-oriented and high technology jobs. However, record shows that trading freely with America's NAFTA partners, Canada and Mexico, has not resulted in a cumulative loss of manufacturing jobs. Instead, from 1994–2000, 14 million new American jobs were reported. The unemployment rate in America fell from 6 percent to 3.9 percent (1994–April 2000). The number of manufacturing jobs in America remained steady, employing 18.3 million people in 1994 and 18.4 million in 1999, which represents 14 percent of the total American workforce. On balance, not only has NAFTA not resulted in a loss of factory jobs in the United States, but it has not led to a loss in real wages for manufacturing workers.

Free trade transmits more than just physical goods or services to people. It also transmits ideas and values. A culture of freedom can flourish whenever a great society, as economist Adam Smith termed it, emerges with the self-confidence to open itself to an inflow of goods and the ideas and practices accompanying them. A culture of freedom can become both the cornerstone and capstone of economic prosperity. One reason why the United States did so much better economically than Europe for more than two centuries is that America had free movement of goods and services while the European countries "protected" themselves from their neighbors. To appreciate the magnitudes involved, try to imagine how much your personal standard of living would suffer if you were not allowed to buy any goods or services that originated outside your home state.

In conclusion, we see that free trade agreements are essential to our nation's prosperity. Without government to forge trade relationships with other countries, our businesses would not be able to reach foreign markets and expand the market share through innovation and competition allowing the consumers and American workforce to benefit from these conditions.

Workers Are Also Consumers, and Protectionism Drives Up Costs for All Consumers

Zornitsa Kutlina-Dimitrova and Csilla Lakatos

Zornitsa Kutlina-Dimitrova is a senior economist in the Chief Trade Economist Unit of the European Commission. Csilla Lakatos is an economist at the World Bank and an expert on applied statistical analysis.

2016 was the fifth consecutive year with merchandise trade growth below 3 percent, much lower than the pre-crisis average of 7 percent. Despite the cyclical recovery observed in 2017, subdued trade growth in the post-crisis period reflects a number of factors. On the one hand, weak global demand is associated with post-crisis legacies in advanced economies, deteriorating terms of trade for commodity exporters and the transition to slower growth in China. On the other hand, longer-term trends have also not favoured trade growth. As a result, the long-run income elasticity of trade has been on the decline (World Bank 2015; Constantinescu et al. 2015), reflecting a shift in demand toward nontradables and services attributable to aging populations, a slowing expansion of global value chains, and the diminishing pace of trade liberalization (IMF 2016). The post-crisis weakness in arm's length trade—trade between unaffiliated firms—has also had a negative impact of trade growth (Lakatos and Ohnsorge 2017).

Not only has stalled trade liberalization been weighing on trade growth, but the post-crisis period has seen an increase in the number of newly introduced protectionist measures. The World Trade Organization (WTO) recently warned about this worrying trend, highlighting that the rate of new trade restrictive measures

"The Global Costs of Protectionism", by Zornitsa Kutlina-Dimitrova and Csilla Lakatos, The World Bank Group, December 14, 2017. http://documents.worldbank.org/curated /en/962781513281198572/pdf/WPS8277.pdf. Licensed under CC BY 3.0 IGO.

introduced by G20 countries in 2016 reached the highest monthly average since 2009 (21 new measures a month), outnumbering measures aimed at facilitating trade (WTO 2016). Similarly, based on a broader definition of protectionist measures, the most recent *Global Trade Alert* (*GTA*) report reveals that despite the recent tapering off in the number of new protectionist measures, the stock of trade barriers in force has been steadily on the rise (Evenett and Fritz 2017). Among these measures, increases in import tariffs account for close to one-fifth of barriers to trade imposed since 2009.

In the current economic environment characterized by subdued potential growth and antiglobalization rhetoric, the risk of beggar-thy-neighbour trade policies has risen. This was highlighted by the recent failure of G20 economies to renew their long-standing commitment to free trade and pledge to resist all forms of protectionism at the last Finance Ministers meeting in March 2017. An increase in within-country income inequality during the period of rapid globalization has fuelled an intense debate about the benefits of trade liberalization and immigration in many advanced economies. Ongoing structural changes in the multilateral trading system and the international communities' response to them will be crucial in shaping the future dynamics of trading relations. If these changes are accompanied by an upward spiral of beggar-thy-neighbour protectionist measures, they could result in the erosion of efforts during decades of trade liberalization and the corrosion of the multilateral rules-based system that's been under construction since the mid-1940s.

While politically attractive in the short run, protectionist measures can have large negative repercussions. As a historical precedent, the implementation of retaliatory trade barriers in response to the Great Depression contributed to wiping out around two-thirds of world trade between 1929 and 1933 (Crucini and Kahn 1996; Madsen 2001). Unilateral increases in trade restrictions will most likely be met with retaliatory measures and, eventually, result in sizable increases in worldwide tariffs.

Such an increase in global protectionism is likely to have wide-ranging, economy-wide consequences not only for consumers, but also producers (firms), government, investment and trade flows. First, an increase in tariffs will translate into an effective increase in the price of imported goods for consumers, reducing their purchasing power and limiting the availability of imported goods. Tariffs have been found to disproportionately impact low-income households as these spend more on traded goods as a share of their income (Fajgelbaum and Khandelwal 2016; Furman et al. 2017). Due to their regressive nature, an increase in tariffs is likely to have adverse distributional effects and negatively impact poverty and income inequality. Second, the increase in the price of imported intermediate inputs will force firms to source their inputs from more expensive domestic markets and potentially pass on the increases in costs to the consumer. This in turn will impact [the] firm's hiring decisions and potentially spill over to changes in wages. Furthermore, given the international fragmentation of production and complex value chains, tariffs may result in cascading trade costs as intermediate goods cross borders multiple times through the stages of production (Diakantoni et al. 2017; Rouzet and Mirodout 2013; World Bank 2017b). Third, the increase in the price of imported capital goods is likely to weigh on investment and disproportionately impact low-income countries (LICs), which rely heavily on imports of machinery and capital goods (World Bank 2017b).

These wide-ranging costs of protectionism can be summarized by a statement made in 1994 by Peter Sutherland, the Director General of the General Agreement on Tariffs and Trade (GATT): "It is high time that governments made clear to consumers just how much they pay—in the shops and as taxpayers—for decisions to protect domestic industries from import competition. Virtually all protection means higher prices. And someone has to pay; either the consumer or, in the case of intermediate goods, another producer. The result is a drop in real income and an inability to buy other products and services."[1]

[…]

Global Rise in Trade Protectionism

The 2008–2009 financial crisis triggered fears of a potential worldwide protectionist spiral (Baldwin and Evenett 2009) and worries of a shift away from the use of traditional trade policy instruments such as import tariffs toward "murky" forms of protectionism.[2] The post-crisis period has indeed seen a steady increase in the number of protectionist measures, which add up to a yearly average of more than 800 new harmful interventions (Evenett and Fritz 2017). The use of murky forms of protectionism has also been on the rise, although traditional trade barriers are still the most predominant policy instrument used. Increases in import tariffs account for close to one-fourth of new barriers to trade introduced since 2009. Other measures, such as anti-dumping duties which also translate into effective increases in applied tariffs are the second most used adding up to more than one-tenth of all new measures.

The WTO recently warned about the global rise in trade protectionism observed in G20 countries and showed that, albeit at a moderate rate, trade restrictions in G20 economies have been rising (WTO 2017) … Based on a broader definition of protectionist measures, the latest *Global Trade Alert* report shows that countries introduced 659 new trade-restrictive measures in 2016 (Evenett and Fritz 2017). The trend seems to continue in 2017 where the number of harmful measures implemented until September reached 335. Since the beginning of the financial crisis, 7,027 discriminatory interventions have been implemented.

Sectors most commonly impacted by protectionist measures are metals, machinery and chemicals which together account for 7 of the top 10 most affected sectors. Barriers that affect agricultural and food sectors have also been gaining prominence and are likely to disproportionately impact exports of the poorest countries which are highly dependent on agricultural production and exports (Evenett and Fritz 2017).

Of all protectionist measures, increases in import tariffs are the most frequently used, accounting for more than one-fifth of all measures introduced since the start of the financial crisis. The total value of imports affected by tariff increases stands at US$684 billion for the period 2009–2017 (Evenett and Fritz 2017). Accounting for multiple tariff increases of the same tariff line, the total value of imports affected would increase to US$864 billion.

The distortive impact of discriminatory trade instruments depends on the length of the period for which they were in force. Evidence shows that of the 1,159 import tariff measures assessed as discriminatory (red), 42 percent were put in place for more than 1 year, 12 percent for more than 2 years and 9 percent for more than 3 years.

Although the number of newly introduced barriers to trade has tapered off in 2017, the risk of protectionism continues to be a major source of concern. This was highlighted by the recent failure of G20 economies to renew their long-standing commitment to free trade and pledge to resist all forms of protectionism at the last Finance Ministers meeting in March 2017.

[…]

Conclusions

At their meeting in March 2017, G20 Finance Ministers failed to renew their long-standing commitment to free trade and pledge to resist all forms of protectionism. If mounting anti-globalization pressures and rising protectionist sentiment culminate in an upward spiral in beggar-thy-neighbour trade policies, they could result in the erosion of efforts during decades of trade liberalization and the corrosion of the multilateral rules-based system that has been under construction since the mid-1940s.

While in some cases protectionist measures are politically attractive in the short run, these can have large negative repercussions over the medium and long run. This paper aims to highlight the wide-ranging costs of protectionism and implicitly the benefits of free trade in two scenarios.

First, what if all WTO members withdrew their tariff commitments from existing unilateral preferential schemes as well as bilateral/regional trade agreements coupled with an increase in the cost of traded services? Although for now such a scenario is purely hypothetical, mounting anti-globalization pressures and rising protectionist sentiment in advanced economies come as a result of widespread doubts about the benefits from free trade. We estimate that such an increase in worldwide protectionism would result in worldwide welfare losses that amount to 0.3 percent or US$211 billion relative to the baseline after three years. An important share of these losses is likely to be concentrated in regions that benefit from important preferential tariffs in their export markets such as East Asia and Pacific and Latin America and the Caribbean and which together account for close to three-quarters of the global decline in welfare. Highlighting the importance of preferences and the value of decades of trade liberalization, the impact on global trade is estimated to be much more pronounced with a decline by 2.1 percent or more than US$606 billion relative to the baseline by 2020.

Second, what if WTO members increased tariffs up to the legally allowed bound rates coupled with an increase in the cost of traded services? This would translate into global welfare losses of 0.8 percent or US$634 billion relative to the baseline after three years. Similarly, global household consumption is found to decrease by 0.9 percent corresponding to a loss of US$445 billion. The distortion to trade flows would be significant with decline by 9 percent or more than US$2.6 trillion relative to the baseline after three years.

Notes

1. Cited in Manzella Trade Communications (2004).

2. Murky forms of protectionism were defined as those that do not necessarily violate WTO obligations but are legitimate abuses of discretion and hurt the commercial interests of trading partners. Examples of these are bailout and stimulus packages or "green protectionism," see also Cernat and Madsen (2011).

The Benefits of Free Trade Far Outweigh the Costs, Including for Workers

Ana Revenga and Anabel Gonzales

Ana Revenga is an economist currently serving as a senior fellow at the Brookings Institution, where she is a member of the Global Economy and Development Program. Anabel Gonzales is a former Costa Rican government official and senior director of the World Bank's Global Practice on Trade and Competitiveness. She is a member of the World Economic Forum's Council on Trade and Investment.

In the ongoing debate about the benefits of trade, we must not lose sight of a vital fact. Trade and global integration have raised incomes across the world, while dramatically cutting poverty *and* global inequality.

Within some countries, trade has contributed to rising inequality, but that unfortunate result ultimately reflects the need for stronger safety nets and better social and labor programs, not trade protection.

Merchandise trade as a share of world GDP grew from around 30 percent in 1988 to around 50 percent in 2013. In this period of rapid globalization, average income grew by 24 percent globally, the global poverty headcount ratio declined from 35% to 10.7%, and the income of the bottom 40 percent of the world population increased by close to 50 percent.

This big picture evidence is buttressed by compelling micro-econometric studies on pro-poor income and consumption gains.

- The 2001, US-Vietnam free trade agreement reduced poverty in Vietnam by increasing wage premiums in export sectors, spurring job reallocation from agriculture, forestry and fishing into manufacturing, and stimulating enterprise job growth.

"Trade Has Been a Global Force for Less Poverty and Higher incomes," by Ana Revenga and Anabel Gonzalez, The World Bank Group, February 2, 2017. Reprinted by permission.

- A study of 27 industrial and 13 developing countries finds that shutting off trade would deprive the richest 10 percent of 28 percent of their purchasing power, but the poorest 10 percent would lose 63 percent because they buy relatively more imported goods.
- In many developing countries, export growth has been associated with greater gender equality. Exporting firms generally employ a significantly higher share of women than non-exporters. In Cambodia's export-oriented garment sector, which is one of the main providers of wage employment in Cambodia, 85 percent of all workers are women.

A retreat from global integration would erode these gains, especially in developing countries. For example, abandoning existing agreements in the Americas would have particularly large negative welfare effects in countries like Mexico (4 to 9 percent), El Salvador (2 to 5 percent), and Honduras (2 to 5 percent), according to early research at the World Bank.

Within countries there are invariably losers as well as winners from trade and globalization. Households are likely to be affected differently depending on their physical and human capital endowments, their consumption patterns, and their incomes. Among developing countries, which we study most closely at the World Bank, there are countries where the direct effect of trade on the wage distribution has been equalizing (e.g. Brazil), and others where it has been un-equalizing (e.g. Mexico). Trade also reduced the (relative) wages of the poor in India in the 1990s, so that poverty decreased less in rural districts more exposed to trade liberalization.

Work-in-progress by some of our colleagues in the World Bank's Research Group seeks to quantify the potential tradeoff between the efficiency gains and inequality costs of trade liberalization using household survey data from 53 low and middle income countries (Artuc, Porto and Rijkers, "Trading-off the Income Gains and the Inequality Costs of Trade Policy," mimeo: World Bank, 2017, in progress). In spite of heterogeneity in the distributional impacts, hard trade-offs are found only in a relatively small number of countries (such as Burundi, Nigeria and Gambia). In the vast majority of countries (including Egypt, Pakistan, and South Africa) trade liberalization significantly raises incomes with at most trivial inequality costs.

Despite the potentially negative effects of trade on some, what happens to final incomes and hence to inequality, however, is not a given. Between 1990 and 2010, a period of rapid globalization, inequality (measured by the Gini index) increased in the United States from 43 to 47 but fell in Denmark from 31 to 26.

Consider why. US workers concentrated in communities which face high volumes of Chinese imports have experienced fewer jobs and falling wages. And yet, the US Trade Adjustment Assistance (TAA) program falls short of the challenge of helping people get back on their feet. The US spends just 0.1% of GDP on all its active labor market polices while the OECD average is 0.6%. Second, the TAA is designed to help only workers suffering direct trade-related job losses but wages losses are not limited to workers who are employed in import competing sectors. Third, the TAA requires active participation of eligible workers in retraining programs but many less educated and older workers, who are worst affected, fail to qualify because they have often already withdrawn from the labor force.

In Denmark, trade liberalization and offshoring also contributed to a decrease in low skill wages, and increase in high skill wages, thus potentially widening inequality. However, the Danish labor assistance system (called Flexicurity) may have helped to avoid any significant increase in inequality. The system targets all workers suffering from job losses, not just workers in sectors exposed to trade and offshoring shocks, and deals with any negative labor market shock, not just relating to trade. The system is based on: a flexible labor market allowing employers to hire and fire relatively easily; a generous unemployment benefit system; and strong activation policies encouraging job search and enhancing workers' employability.

In countries where trade has created losers, policies that redistribute some of the gains from winners to losers are needed to ensure the benefits of trade are widely shared. They also need policies to better equip workers to benefit from the opportunities offered by trade. Better and more generous safety nets and other social protection policies, and more investments in skill acquisition, are the answer. Not protectionist trade policies that will blunt the engine of growth that has delivered prosperity for millions around the world. This insight guides our work in a World Bank Group dedicated to ending extreme poverty and boosting shared prosperity for all.

CHAPTER 3

Does Global Trade Reduce Benefits of a Local Cultural and Economic System?

What Is Globalization and What Are Its Effects?

Lumen Learning

Lumen Learning is an education technology company that develops low cost products and open educational resources (OER) for colleges and universities to enhance affordability and access to education in the United States.

Globalization is a term used to describe how countries, people and businesses around the world are becoming more interconnected, as forces like technology, transportation, media, and global finance make it easier for goods, services, ideas and people to cross traditional borders and boundaries. Globalization offers both benefits and challenges. It can provide tremendous opportunity for economic growth to improve the quality of life for many people. It can also lead to challenges with the welfare of workers, economies, and the environment as businesses globalize and shift their operations between countries to take advantage of lower costs of doing business in other world regions.

Globalization, Economic Growth and Market Opportunity

Globalization creates opportunities for many countries to experience economic growth. Economic growth is the increase in the amount of the goods and services produced by an economy over time. It is conventionally measured as a percentage change in the Gross Domestic Product (GDP) or Gross National Product (GNP). These two measures, which are calculated slightly differently, total the amounts paid for the goods and services that a country produced. As an example of measuring economic growth, a country that creates $9,000,000 in goods and services in 2010 and then creates $9,090,000 in 2011 has a nominal economic growth rate of 1 percent for 2011.

A way of classifying the economic growth of countries is to divide them into three groups: (a) industrialized, (b) developing, and (c) less-developed nations.

- Industrialized nations have economies characterized by a healthy climate for private enterprise (business) and a consumer orientation, meaning the business climate focuses on meeting consumers' long-term wants and needs. These nations have high literacy rates, modem technology, and higher per capita incomes. Historically, industrialized nations include United States, Canada, Japan, South Korea, Australia, New Zealand, and most Western European nations. Newly industrialized countries include Russia and most other eastern European countries, Turkey, South Africa, China, India, and Brazil, among others.

- Less-developed nations, also known as least-developed countries (LDCs) have extensive poverty, low per capita income and standards of living, low literacy rates, and very limited technology. Often these nations lack strong government, financial, and economic systems to support a healthy business community. Their economies tend to be focused on agriculture and production of raw materials (such as the mining and timber industries). There are many less-developed nations in the world, with most located in Africa and Asia.

- Developing nations are those that are making the transition from economies based on agricultural and raw-materials production to industrialized economies. They exhibit rising levels of education, technology, and per capita incomes. Governments in these nations typically have made strong progress to improve the climate for business in order to attract business and economic investment. There is a growing list of developing nations, including many countries in Latin America and Asia.

Usually, the most significant marketing opportunities exist among the industrialized nations, as they have higher levels of income, one of the necessary ingredients for the formation of markets. However, market saturation for many products already exists in these nations.

The developing countries, on the other hand, have growing population bases, and although most import a limited number of goods and services from other countries, longer-term growth potential exists in these nations. Often, marketers in developing nations must be educators, using marketing techniques to [educate] populations about unfamiliar, new products and services and the benefits they provide. As the degree of economic development increases, so does the sophistication of the marketing effort focused on a country.

Benefits of Globalism for Business

Those in favor of globalization theorize that a wider array of products, services, technologies, medicines, and knowledge will become available, and that these developments will have the potential to reach significantly larger customer bases. This means larger volumes of sales and exchange, larger growth rates in GDP, and more empowerment of individuals and political systems through the acquisition of additional resources and capital. These benefits of globalization are viewed as utilitarian, providing the best possible benefits for the largest number of people.

For global companies, often referred to as multinational corporations (MNCs), common benefits of expanding into developing markets include unsaturated demand for new products, lower labor costs, less expensive natural resources, and other inputs to products. Technological developments have made doing business internationally much more convenient than in the past. MNCs seek to benefit from globalism by selling goods in multiple countries, as well as sourcing production in areas that can produce goods more profitably. In other words, organizations choose to operate internationally either because they can achieve higher levels of revenue or because they can achieve a lower cost structure within their operations.

MNCs look for opportunities to realize economies of scale by mass-producing goods in markets that have substantially cheaper costs for labor or other inputs. Or they may look for economies of scope, through horizontal expansion into new geographic markets. If successful, both of these strategies lead to business growth, with stronger margins and/or larger revenues. There is particularly strong opportunity for business growth in markets where strong economic growth is also projected. In these areas, incomes are rising. In many cases, local populations can now afford goods and services that were previously out-of-reach, including many goods produced in industrialized countries. Global companies stand to capture stronger growth and profitability if they can make headway into these markets.

At the same time, international operations contain innate risk in developing new opportunities in foreign countries.

Challenges of Globalism for Business

Along with arguments supporting the benefits of a more globally connected economy, critics question the ethics and long-term feasibility of profits captured through global expansion. Some argue that the expansion of global trade creates unfair exchanges between larger and smaller economies. They argue that MNCs and industrialized economies capture significantly more value because they have more financial leverage and can dictate advantageous terms of exchange, which end up victimizing developing nations. Critics also raise concerns about damage to the environment, decreased food safety, unethical labor practices in sweatshops, increased consumerism, and the weakening of traditional cultural values.

As MNCs do business in new global markets, they may encounter several significant challenges:

- Ethical Business Practices: Arguably the most substantial of the challenges faced by MNCs, ethical business practices in areas such as labor, product safety, environmental stewardship, corruption, and regulatory compliance have historically played a dramatic role in the success or failure of global players. For example, Nike's brand image was hugely damaged by reports that it utilized sweatshops and low-wage workers in developing countries. In some nations, particularly those without a strong rule of law, bribing public officials (e.g., paying them off with gifts or money) is relatively common by those seeking favorable business terms. Although national and international laws exist to crack down on bribery and corruption, some businesspeople and organizations are pressured to go along with locally accepted practices. Maintaining the highest ethical standards while operating in any nation is an important consideration for all MNCs.

- Organizational Structure: Another significant hurdle is the ability to efficiently and effectively incorporate new regions within the value chain and corporate structure. International expansion requires enormous capital investments in many cases, along with the development of a specific strategic business unit (SBU) in order to manage these accounts and operations. Finding a way to capture value despite this fixed organizational investment is an important initiative for global corporations.

- Public Relations: Public image and branding are critical components of most businesses. Building this public relations potential in a new geographic region is an enormous challenge, both in effectively localizing the message and in the capital expenditures necessary to create momentum.

- Leadership: It can be difficult for businesses to find effective organizational leadership with the appropriate knowledge and skills to approach a given geographic market successfully. For every geography worldwide, unique sets of strategies and approaches apply to language, culture, business networks, management style, and so forth. Attracting talented managers with high intercultural competence is a critical step in developing an effective global strategy.

- Legal and Regulatory Structure: Every nation has unique laws and regulations governing business. MNCs need access to legal expertise to help them understand in-country laws and comply with applicable regulations. It is important for businesses to understand the legal and regulatory climate for their industry and type of organization before entering a new market, so that this information can be factored into the business case and strategic decisions about where and how to expand globally, as well as strategic and operational planning to ensure profitability.

For organizations operating in developing and less-developed countries, additional challenges can arise, particularly in the following areas:

- Infrastructure: Infrastructure includes the basic physical and organizational structures needed for a society to operate and for an economy to function. It can be generally defined as the set of interconnected structural elements that provide a framework supporting an entire structure of development, such as roads, bridges, water supply, sewers, electrical grids, telecommunications, and so forth. It also includes organizational structures such as a stable government, property rights, judicial system, banking and financial systems, and basic social services such as schools and hospitals. A country's infrastructure will help determine the ease of doing business within that nation. For example, a country with poor road conditions and intense traffic may not be the best place to conduct business that requires goods to be transported from city to city by land. Poor infrastructure makes it difficult for businesses to operate effectively because they have to shoulder additional cost and risk to make up for what the country's society does not provide.

- Technology: The level of technological development of a nation affects the attractiveness of doing business there, as well as the type of operations that are possible. Companies may encounter a variety of technological challenges doing business in foreign countries, such as training workers on unfamiliar equipment; poor transportation systems that increase production and distribution costs; poor communication facilities and infrastructure; challenges with technology literacy; lack of reliable access to broad-band Internet and related technologies that facilitate business planning, implementation, and control.

All of these factors—both benefits and challenges—should go into decisions about whether and how to expand globally. Marketing, along with other business functions, can be affected for better or for worse by the advantages and disadvantages posed by global business. Organizational leaders must consider carefully how to balance costs and risks against the potential for gain and growth.

Globalization and Islam

Mohd Abbas Abdul Razak

Mohd Abbas Abdul Razak is an assistant professor of fundamental and interdisciplinary studies at the International Islamic University in Malaysia. His research focuses on the cross-cultural analysis of educational and religious institutions, as well as conceptions of psychology in Western and Islamic culture.

The Golden Age of the Muslims

During the Golden Age of Islam (750–1258), Muslims were in the forefront in conquering knowledge through scientific research, exploration and expeditions. In their pursuit of mastering new knowledge and technology, Muslims were prepared and open to the idea of learning all that is positive from the earlier civilizations. As such they borrowed ideas from the Indians, Persians and Greeks as a way of enriching their own civilization. While pioneering into many scientific research works, Muslims were also equally interested in mastering Greek philosophical thoughts and the human sciences. The zeal they had for philosophy brought them closer to the ideas of the ancient philosophers like Socrates (469BC–399BC), Plato (427BC–347BC), Aristotle (384BC–322BC) and others.[1,2]

In realizing the fact that not all ideas of the Greek philosophers were acceptable to their Islamic worldview, early Muslim scholars used the approach of adopt, adapt and assimilate or integrate. Through this methodology, the early Muslim scholars took all those ideas which were non-contradictory to their religious values and faith. The scholars of the Golden Age of Islam not only borrowed ideas from others but they went on to further expand and come up with some new, original and innovative ideas. This was the spirit and culture of learning that was prevalent during the early Muslim era of knowledge expansion and exploration. Similarly, Western

"Globalization and Its Impact on Education and Culture," by Mohd Abbas Abdul Razak, International Digital Organization for Scientific Information, *World Journal of Islamic History and Civilization*, 1 (1): 59-69, 2011. Reprinted by permission.

scholars too had borrowed ideas from Muslim scholars during the Golden Age of the Muslims. Europeans learnt philosophical ideas of the Greek from the translated and annotated works done by the Muslim scholars. Moreover, they also learnt from many pioneering works done by Muslim scholars and scientists in the field of medicine, astronomy, chemistry, mathematics, algebra, trigonometry, etc. At the moment, only a few Western scholars duly acknowledge the great contribution made by the Muslims in inspiring and introducing the West towards science and scientific explorations.[3,4]

Much of the scholastic works accomplished during the Golden Age of the Muslims were either diminished or came to a standstill during the Mongols invasion of Baghdad led by Hulagu Khan (1217–1265) in 1258. During the Mongols invasion, not only great numbers of Muslims were butchered, but also their libraries with large volumes of books and original manuscripts were burnt to ashes. The era between the fall of Baghdad and the European colonization of Muslim lands in the 18th and 19th centuries kept the Muslim scholars occupied in their own polemic in the area of Islamic jurisprudence. In addition to this, they were also busy bickering and discrediting one another.[3] This condition held them back from advancing any further in the field of science and technology. This situation persisted for very long in the Muslim world even during the dawn of the Industrial Revolution in Britain. During the Industrial Revolution, the West had managed to advance many steps ahead in the areas of science and research, leaving the Muslim world lagging behind. The Muslims who earlier did many pioneering works in the field of science either produced little or showed no progress in their research works while the Europeans made giant strides in science during the Industrial Revolution.[5]

In modern times, the brunt of Western subjugation on Muslim countries is still obviously seen in how these countries are impoverished and left behind in the many sectors of nation building. The educational and technological gaps created by colonization are huge and noticeable when compared to the rich and affluent countries in the West. Though at the moment all Muslim countries are liberated and some in spite of having rich natural resources is still no where closer of being on par with the advanced nations of the world. In a way colonization has also made Muslim countries very much dependent on the West, particularly in the areas of knowledge, science and technology. In turn, this state of dependence has given the West an advantage in maintaining their control over their former colonies from afar. Colonization in the modern era is no longer physical in nature but more of controlling the hearts and minds of the people in the developing and third world countries. This new form of colonization, better known as neo-colonialism is done via the use of modern means of telecommunication that do not require the colonizers to be physically present in the countries of their interest. The latest form of control used by the West in imposing its supremacy over the East is through globalization. Many experts in area of globalization indicated that this term actually refers to re-colonization in the subtle form.

[…]

Impact on Culture

The proponents of globalization argue that it has brought rapid development to many parts of the world by bringing people in the third world countries out of their backwardness and old ideas, and put them on par with the people of the developed countries in the world. According to Chandra [Muzaffar], the proponents of globalization highlight the following positive aspects of globalization:

1. Foreign direct investment (FDI) has helped to reduce poverty by creating jobs and improving incomes.
2. The expansion of trade and foreign investment has accelerated social mobility and strengthened the middle class.

3. New communication and information technology have helped disseminate knowledge in many fields of study and disciplines.

4. Communication is cheaper and easier. Costs of telephone [calls] as well as travel have fallen.

5. This makes it easier to understand one another. Communities, although heterogeneous, can be more cooperative now and there are more means of understanding each other.

6. Globalization makes it possible for humanity to have compassion for each other when calamities—natural or man-made—affect others.

7. Issues such as human rights, public accountability and problems faced by women are brought to the fore and addressed.

8. The rights of women are highlighted and the problems many women face are now addressed.

9. All of these are conducive to religious teachings.[13]

In the Muslim world, scholars can generally be classified into two main groups with regards to the issue of globalization. The first group claims that globalization is not too bad an idea as it has some positive contribution in terms of trade and direct foreign investment creating plentiful job opportunities in the underdeveloped and developing nations. The second group deems globalization as bad because it is a Western idea or ideology that works well to their benefit. According to this group, globalization is actually colonization in disguise. They further believe that the West has not changed in their mindset in their ambition like in the past which brought them ploughing the waves to subjugate the East in greed of power, riches and dominance over the weak and downtrodden. Through their direct subjugation of the East and Africa, they have managed to plunder all the wealth of the under-privileged countries. Globalization as seen by these scholars is nothing new than the old colonization, except it is done in a more subtle manner, from distance by using sophisticated media like cable and satellite TV, internet and other modern means of communications. In describing the nature and contents of globalization designed by the West, Mohd Kamal has candidly explained in these words:

> *Facing the challenges of globalization with all the negative impacts of Americanization, secularization, materialism, neo-imperialism, debt-bondage to World Bank and IMF, unilateralism, militant liberal capitalism, global media conglomerates' manipulation and deception, impoverishment and homogenization of culture, bullying by the powerful, imposed liberalization, dominance of the global market, international and regional competition, commodification of education, environmental degradation, moral decadence, high tech crime, violence and war—all these and more at a time when the Muslim world is divided, weak and poor.*[14]

Going deep into contemplation and analysis of what has been stated by Mohd Kamal will reveal that globalization has brought Western culture and way of life to the East and to the rest of the world. At many times these values are atheistic in nature that does not regard the Supremacy of God Almighty. Through globalization, secularism practiced by the West is also transported to the homes and minds of the people in the East, disrupting their Islamic and Eastern family core-values that are already there in existence. Secularism is a way of life that separates things and actions into two—all that belongs to God and all that belongs to the state. The two states of affair cannot mix. The dichotomy that is prevalent in their everyday life gives people in the West to think of God only when they are in the places of worship and when they are elsewhere, they can behave and do anything and everything that suit their selfish desires. Such a philosophy of life is very opposed and contradictory to the Islamic and Eastern life style where people live very much attached to their religious beliefs.

Another important thing about globalization that is contradictory to the religion of Islam is the Western idea that states education should be value-free. Knowledge and education are sought for knowledge and it does not link the individual with God almighty. In Islam, knowledge is sought for self-improvement that humbles down man in the presence of his Creator. Knowledge is sought for the enlightenment of the human soul that brings man closer to God. In contrast to the Islamic concept of seeking knowledge, most people in the West believe that knowledge is value-free. Other than this, the Western attitude of non-judgmental in the things they see, acquire, experience and assess is not applicable in the context of the Muslim society. Islam calls on the Muslims to take a stand by being judgmental. One has to be clear in his mind as to what are the things that have been approved and shunned by the Qur'an and the Sunnah with regards to the human relationship. By referring to the religious guidelines, one can easily distinguish between what is good and permissible and what is bad and should be avoided.

Parents, teachers and religious leaders in many Muslim countries fear that the call by proponents of globalization that states free flow of information, can be really detrimental to the family and social structure of the Islamic and Eastern society. They fear that globalization transported via the internet and other modern means of telecommunication will somehow transport the Western hedonistic life-style. Many of these ideas and ideology that come along through the media and internet bring along ideology and way of life that are contradictory to the Islamic belief system and Eastern culture. One particular area that is feared by parents, among the many things that come from the West, is sexual perversion. Under this category, homosexuality, lesbianism and other forms of sexual perversion are something that cannot be allowed and practiced in Muslim countries. In Islam, these forms of human relationship are not acceptable under the Islamic Syariah (Islamic Law). In the West, the rights of the individual for his/her desires to be fulfilled which do not cause harm to another human beings is allowed though this might go against their religious beliefs. Islam forbids homosexual and lesbian marriages, and describes this sort of relationship is seen as an adulteration to the institution of family that has been thing sacred and ordained by God Almighty.

Besides that, children if left unchecked to use the internet are exposed to the danger of entering into websites that display pornography and other unhealthy and unethical information. It is believed that such information can corrupt their innocent and tender hearts and minds. It is feared that children that gain access to such information on the internet will be trapped in a vicious circle that might lead them into other social ills.

The exponents of globalization have also highlighted that globalization abolishes cultural differences among the diverse and multi-lingual societies of the world. Globalization promotes homogenous society changing the world of its heterogeneous nature that has been created by God Almighty. The present scenario in the world clearly shows the process of homogenization is taking place and this is an ongoing thing. Dominance of English language as an important international language, obsession for American lifestyle in terms of their fast food like KFC and McDonald, preference over American banded items like clothing, music and movies are clear indicators of the homogenization of societies in the world is taking place.

How Should Muslims Respond to Globalization?

Globalization has started without being realized by a large section of the Islamic Ummah. Since the tidal waves of globalization have already started to touch the shores of the Islamic countries, efforts need to be taken to prevent them from causing damage to their faith and Islamic way of life. As it has been understood from the preceding discussion that globalization is irreversible and inevitable the Muslims have no choice but to prepare and safeguard them to confront its onslaughts that come from all directions.

In realizing that something need to be done, Malaysia's former Prime Minister Tun Mahathir has said the following in one of his addresses to the Islamic Ummah on the issue on globalization:

Muslim countries and Muslim governments have a duty to ensure that globalization will not result in the marginalization of their countries as happened with the Industrial Revolution and Industrial Age. We cannot afford it this time. If once again we miss this opportunity to keep pace with the radical and rapid advances now being made with technology and the sciences, and the changes they cause to the world's perceptions of things, the new ideas and concepts in human and international relations; if we miss all these and fail to handle them, then we will not only be marginalized, but be dominated and hegemonised permanently.[5]

According to Tun Mahathir, during the last Industrial Revolution that took place in the West, the European nations used their creative intelligence and came up with a lot of breakthrough in the areas of science, technology and medicine. They made many discoveries with the creations of many items that became very essential for a better living for the modern man. The many machineries discovered by scientists and scholars benefited them in making them as advanced nations in the world later on. While the Europeans were making new discoveries, the scenario in Arabia was quite different. The Arabs at that time were still debating on minor issues of fiqh (jurisprudence) and other issues regarding which school of thought (mazhab) is more superior to the other. That time of the Arabs compared to the Golden Age of Islam, the Muslims were creative, productive and prolific and contributed a lot in the fields of philosophy, astronomy, medicine, algebra, etc., which later benefited by the Europeans. Baghdad, Cordova, Syria and Egypt became centers for knowledge and learning which invited the Europeans to flock around in these centers and to learn from the scholastic works produced by Muslim scholars.

Tun Mahathir's call is a reminder for the Muslims not to ignore and stay away from the events and progress that are taking place in the area of information technology, multi-media, e-learning, e-commerce, etc. If the Muslims choose to stay isolated from others in this era of globalization then the Muslims will be the ones who will be left alone and become the losers compared to the rest of the world. A wise thing to do by the Muslims is to be active in mastering the new technology and use it for a good purpose that can bring progress, development and economic benefit to themselves and for the rest of humanity.

Other form of safeguarding the Ummah that can be undertaken by Islamic countries in this era of globalization is by cutting down on their dependency on the West in terms of technology, which also includes in the area of multimedia and software development. Mental dependency on the West is a form of colonization. So long as the Muslim countries and leaders depend on the West for technology and expertise, they will be subjugated and put under their control. Islam as a way of life of the Muslims does not encourage them to be ruled by others and live under the hegemony and dictates of others who preach against their religion.[15]

Besides that, oil rich Muslim countries should make attempts to re-channel their multi-billion investments from America and Europe to some of the developing and poor Muslim countries in the world. By doing that, it is hoped that the disparities between the rich and poor Muslim countries can be eradicated. This action also confirms what has been emphasized in the Qur'an, that we should help one another, and this is also deemed as a praiseworthy deed in the sight of Allah SWT.

On the question of internet as a powerful tool in disseminating knowledge and information and what should be the Muslims stand on this matter. As there are good and bad in the internet usage, Muslims should be smart to use this tool for getting knowledge and information. They should also use it to their advantage in the promulgation of Islam, although some outside the religion may want to use it for spreading profanity and sexual perversion. Besides that, the internet can also be used to stay connected with the rest of the Ummah living in other parts of the world.

Another important effort that needs the attention of Muslim countries is their willingness to invest in the area of [research] and development. This ability to do research during the Golden Age of Islam brought them to the pinnacle of their success and made European scholars to come to their centers of learning and research. After that period, due to complacency Muslims lost all the good qualities as good researchers to the Europeans. As a result of this, the Ummah started to lag behind the Europeans. Apart from that, colonization which forced Muslims into poverty also in a way made the strength of the Ummah to dwindle drastically. Even after attaining independence from the Western colonial powers, the Muslims have yet to reclaim the status they once had prior to the fall of Baghdad in 1258. In realizing this predicament, Muslims should exert themselves diligently in conducting research. This in turn will break their mental dependency on the West.

In the area of news broadcast, the Muslims cannot rely totally on the Western media like CNN, BBC, ABC and other international news agencies. At the moment, there has been a small breakthrough in the area of news media with the emergence of Al-Jazeera. Before this, the Muslims like the rest of the other nations were all dependent on the Western media to know what is happening in the Islamic world and other regions of the world. Most of the time these Western medias provide a bias reporting of what is happening to the Muslims. Through the manipulation of the media, the West has portrayed the Ummah as one that is dangerous, backward and one that is posing a threat to the world community. All these false reporting and prejudices can be contradicted with the Muslims having their own news media broadcasting the truth by reporting the actual and factual happening in the Muslim world.

All the strength and riches cannot help the Muslims to fight the tides of globalization if the whole Muslim world does not come together as a one united Ummah. The lesson taught by the Qur'an calling the Muslims to get united (Al 'Imran: 103)[16] has yet to be materialized fully by the Muslims ever since that verse was revealed to the Prophet of Islam SAW. Besides this, the Westerners have also taught us that, "United we stand, divided we fall". It seems that the Muslims have not learnt from their bitter experiences of the past living under subjugation and their failures have not taught them lessons to mend their ways to attain the status Allah has mentioned in the Qur'an as the best Ummah (Khaira Ummah). Being united under organization like the OIC (Organization of Islamic Countries) gives the Ummah its lost dignity in the eyes of the other nations of the world. The state of being united makes the Ummah more vocal in sending a common message to the UN when making decision pertaining to the problems faced by the Muslims, be it political or economic. People like Tun Mahathir, Chandra [Muzaffar] and Mohd Kamal believe that the UN, World Bank and IMF are all part of the forces of globalization, working to the advantage of the rich and powerful nations of the world. If the Islamic Ummah is weak and not alert of the forces that are at work to destroy it then it will suffer forever in the hands of the predators of globalization.

Another portent strategy to face globalization by the Islamic Ummah is to strike a balance between the physical development of the nation with the spiritual and moral development of its people. Without the spiritual and moral development all other developments will not guarantee to bring real success and prosperity to the Muslim countries.

Is Globalization Equal to Colonization?

The researcher is of the opinion that, the five definitions provided by Jan Aart Scholte are all true in one way or the other. All these definitions that explain globalization as Internationalization, Liberalization, Universalization, Westernization / Modernization and Deterritorialization when analyzed will reveal the true nature of globalization.

If colonization is to suppress and oppress others to make one nation to stay high and mighty, definitely globalization shares a lot in common with colonization. Globalization is an idea and ideology that comes from the West, is mainly intended to make them rich and to put them high above the Asians, Africans and others. Globalization is in fact colonization in disguise. Using it as a tool and a means, the West intends to control the hearts and minds of the young and old in the underprivileged countries of the world. They control us with a press of a button using the internet, international media and other modern and sophisticated ways of telecommunication.

The manner of controlling the developing and poor nations of the world from far was clearly witnessed during the Asian economic downturn in 1997–1998. Due to the manipulation of the stock-market in the Asian region by Western currency-traders and foreign fund managers, all the "Tiger Economies" like Malaysia, Thailand, South Korea, Indonesia, Philippines and others suffered a lot due to devaluation of their currency. All economic strength built by these countries after their independence within the period of 40–50 years fell significantly making these countries impoverished overnight.[17]

Conclusion

In analyzing the impact of globalization on education, the researcher agrees that it has some good and bad effect on the people in the developing and underdeveloped countries. Education should not be separated from its lofty ideals that aim at producing good individuals as well as good citizens who will have a good relationship with God Almighty, fellow human beings, with the environment (flora and fauna). These countries should invest more in education. Governments in these countries must monitor all institution of higher learning especially the ones established by the West so that they offer affordable education for the people to gain tertiary education.

On the cultural front, good and healthy culture that comes from the West via globalization should be imitated and followed leaving the bad and immoral culture that is detrimental to the existence of the society. The culture of doing research and development, reading and exploring and conquering of new ideas are positive things that we can follow.

The researcher feels that people in the third world countries should not totally reject everything that comes from the West. The people in the East, particularly the Muslims should have an

Open mind to examine all that come from the West and should pick and choose whatever that is relevant to their needs and discard all that are dangerous and harmful to their existence as a community and nation. Certainly the Muslims cannot live in their own enclavement in total seclusion and isolation running away from globalization. They must view globalization as a challenge and look for a solution to overcome this problem. Contribution of a Muslim towards looking for a solution for the betterment of the Islamic Ummah is deemed one form of Jihad in the path of Allah.

References

1. M. Abbas, *Contribution of Iqbal's Dynamic Personality Theory to Islamic Psychology: A Contrastive Analysis With Freud and Selected Mainstream Western Psychology.* Selangor: International Islamic University Malaysia, 2011.

2. I. Rossidy, *An Analysis of al-Attas' and al-Faruqi's Conceptions of Islamization of Knowledge: Implications for Muslim Education.* Selangor: International Islamic University Malaysia, 1998.

3. M. Abbas, *Human nature: A comparative study between western and Islamic psychology.* Selangor: International Islamic University Malaysia, 1997.

4. H. Langgulung, *Beberapa tinjauan dalam pendidikan Islam.* Kuala Lumpur: Penerbitan Pustaka Antara, 1981.

5. M. Mohamed, *Globalisation and the New Realities.* Subang Jaya, Malaysia: Pelanduk Publications (M) Sdn. Bhd, 2003.

6. D. Block and D. Cameron, *Globalization and Language Teaching.* London: UK: Routledge, 2002, pp: 2.

7. J. A. Scholte, retrieved August 10th, 2011. http://www.infed.org/biblio/defining globalization.

8. N. C. Burbules and C.A. Torres, *Globalization and Education.* New York: Routledge, 2000, pp: 3.

9. Online Encyclopedia, retrieved August 10th, 2011. http://education.yahoo.com /reference/ encyclopedia/entry/education.

10. D. Kellner, "Globalization and New Social Movements: Lessons for Critical Theory and Pedagoggy" in *Globalization and Education*, N. C. Burbules and C. A. Torres, eds. New York: Routledge, 2000, pp: 299-321.

11. E. Fromm, *The Art of Living.* London: Thorsons, 1995, pp: 67.

12. D. Walsh, "Plato Meets Technology," *Washington Post*, 14th September 1999, pp: A29.

13. C. Muzaffar, *Globalization and Religion: Some Reflection.* Retrieved October 19, 2004. http://www.islamoline.net.

14. M. K. Hassan, "Setting the Muslim Mindset in Malaysia: Facing the Challenge of Globalization," keynote address delivered at the International Conference on Teaching and Teacher Education, Kuala Lumpur, 16th September, 2003.

15. A. al-Roubaie, *Globalization and the Muslim World*. Shah Alam: Malita Jaya Publishing House, 2002, pp.90-102.

16. "And hold fast, all together, unto the bond with God, and do not draw apart from one another. And remember the blessing which God has bestowed upon you: how, when you were enemies, He brought your hearts together, so that through His blessing you became brethren; and [how, when] you were on the brink of fiery abyss, He saved you from it" (3:103). Translation from M. Assad, *The Message of the Qur'an*. Gibraltar: Dar al-Andalus Limited, 1980, pp: 82-83.

17. M. Mohamad, *The Challenges of Turmoil*. Subang Jaya: Pelanduk Publications (M) Sdn. Bhd., 1998, pp: 7-13.

The Impact of Globalization on Cultural Diversity and Heritage

UNESCO Publications

The Paris-based United Nations Educational, Scientific, and Cultural Organization (UNESCO) supports academic and intellectual efforts to promote the ideals expressed in the United Nations Charter: justice, the rule of law, and respect for human rights.

The diversity of human cultures—the wealth of languages, ideas, beliefs, kinship systems, customs, tools, artistic works, rituals and other expressions they collectively embody—admits of many explanations and interpretations. These range from philosophical considerations, through an emphasis on cultures as emergent systems or in terms of intercultural contacts, to approaches that highlight the complex interactions between cultures and the human habitat. A current consensus regards cultures as systems that continually evolve through internal processes and in contact with the environment and other cultures. What is certain is that no society has ever been frozen in its history, even if some cultures have been viewed as "timeless" from the perspective of others characterized by rapid change.

Cultural diversity, beyond the mere fact of its existence, has aesthetic, moral and instrumental value as the expression of human creativity, the embodiment of human strivings and the sum of humanity's collective experience. In the contemporary world—characterized as it is by space-time compression linked to the speed of new communication and transportation technologies, and by the growing complexity of social interactions and the increasing overlap of individual and collective identities—cultural diversity has become a key concern, amid accelerating globalization

"Investing in Cultural Diversity and Intercultural Dialogue," UNESCO Publications, 2007. Reprinted by permission.

processes, as a resource to be preserved and as a lever for sustainable development.

In the context of the threats to cultural diversity, the international community has adopted a panoply of binding and non-binding instruments covering a wide range of cultural forms, including monuments and natural sites, tangible and intangible heritage, cultural expressions, and intellectual and artistic heritage. These instruments are dedicated to preserving and promoting such testimonies to human creativity as expressions of the common heritage of humankind. Part I of this report reviews some of these safeguarding mechanisms, with reference to the most recent developments. However, its main concern is with the wider phenomenon and multiple aspects of cultural diversity and with the related issue of intercultural dialogue. Indeed, cultural diversity and dialogue are mutually reinforcing, such that the maintenance of cultural diversity is intimately linked to the ability to establish dialogue and the ultimate challenge of cultural diversity is that of intercultural dialogue.

Cultural Diversity

Globalization is not a wholly new phenomenon. Empires throughout history have sought to extend their dominion and influence beyond their immediate horizons. European colonialism reflected a similar imperialist impulse, inaugurating political, social, economic and cultural imbalances that have persisted into the new millennium. Yet contemporary globalization is of a different order to such historical anticipations. Recent decades have witnessed an unprecedented enmeshment of national economies and cultural expressions, giving rise to new challenges and opportunities. Communication networks have shrunk or abolished distance, to the benefit of some and the exclusion of others. Travel has never been so rapid and convenient, while remaining beyond the reach of many. In a world in which the possibilities of intercultural contact have multiplied, linguistic diversity and many other forms of cultural expression are in decline. How then is globalization to be viewed in terms of its impacts on cultural diversity?

Globalization is often conceived as potentially antithetical to cultural diversity, in the sense of leading to the homogenization of cultural models, values, aspirations and lifestyles, to the standardization of tastes, the impoverishment of creativity, uniformity of cultural expressions and so forth. The reality, however, is more complex. While it is true that globalization induces forms of homogenization and standardization, it cannot be regarded as inimical to human creativity, which continues to engender new forms of diversity, constituting a perennial challenge to featureless uniformity.

Cultural Diversity in a Globalizing World

Globalization is often seen as a *unidirectional* and *unidimensional* process, driven by a Western-dominated global market economy and tending to standardize, streamline and transnationalize in ways inimical to cultural diversity. The focus is on the threat posed to local cultural products and practices by globalized consumer goods and services—on how television and video productions are tending to eclipse traditional forms of entertainment, how pop and rock music are drowning out indigenous music, or how convenience food is blunting the appetite for local cuisine. Some forms of cultural diversity are clearly more vulnerable than others. Vernacular languages are recognized as being particularly at risk, notably from the continuing expansion of English but also from the advance of vehicular languages such as Arabic, Hindi, Spanish and Swahili. This process tends to be exponential—as illustrated by the emphasis placed by many parents on schooling their children in vehicular languages at the expense of mastery of their mother tongue.

A Multidirectional and Multidimensional Process

Through the media, globalization conveys an often seductive image of modernity and provides a template for collective ambitions:

salaried employment, the nuclear family, personalized transport, pre-packaged leisure, conspicuous consumption. Most local communities worldwide have been exposed to some extent to the images and consumer practices typical of this Western paradigm, which has now impacted on almost all countries, irrespective of culture, religion, social system and political regime. The adoption of many of its facets is closely linked to rapidly expanding urban living, which now involves some 50 percent of the world's population. Cultural erosion has accordingly become an issue of increasing concern since numerous modes of life are being lost and many cultural forms and expressions are disappearing. There is a widespread sense that globalization is leading to pervasive cultural homogenization, not to say hegemonization by stealth.

There can be no doubt that the development of transnational markets, linked to the rise of consumerism promoted by skillful advertising, is impacting significantly on local cultures, which are finding it difficult to compete in an increasingly global marketplace. In this context, the tendency of enterprises to delocalize to the developing world as part of the liberalization of world trade is creating new consumer patterns in which the juxtaposition of contrasting lifestyles can serve to accelerate cultural change that may be neither welcome nor desirable. When, for example, a multinational corporation decides to transfer its production to a country in the South because of its lower labour costs, the products of Western consumer society begin to circulate domestically, sometimes to the detriment of local cultural models. In these circumstances, local cultures that find it difficult to compete in the global marketplace—but whose value is incommensurable with any market valuation—tend to be the losers, along with the diversity of the cultural manifestations they embody.

This said, the association of globalization with standardization and commodification is often overstated. The assertion that "whatever [the] market touches turns into a consumer commodity; including the things that try to escape its grip" (Bauman, 2005) fails to take account of the complexities inherent in the integration of cultural borrowings. Movements between geo-cultural areas invariably involve translation, mutation and adaptation on the part of the receiving culture, and cultural transfer does not usually take place unilaterally. Globalized media, for instance, are increasingly being appropriated by marginalized and previously voiceless groups in order to advance their social, economic and political claims. Furthermore, many areas of everyday cultural experience prove beyond the reach of the globalized market, such as our deeply rooted sense of national or ethnic identities, our religious or spiritual ties, our community interests, activities and attachments, not to mention our environments and social relationships. Most importantly, cultural commerce is to an ever greater extent a two-way process that takes place in an increasingly complex and interactive international context.

For all these reasons, globalization is best understood as a multidirectional and multidimensional process, evolving simultaneously within the economic, social, political, technological and cultural spheres. It is a complex and rapidly developing network of connections and interdependencies that operate within and between these spheres and exert increasing influence on material, social, economic and cultural life in today's world. Globalization can be described in terms of the increasing "flows" of virtually everything that characterizes contemporary life: capital, commodities, knowledge, information, ideas, people, beliefs and so on. These flows—transiting essentially through the media, communication networks and commerce—consist of an ever-increasing volume of cultural goods, services and communications, including language and educational content. While this cultural traffic has tended to move along a mainly North-South axis, the rise of powerful new economies (in particular, the BRICs, i.e. Brazil, Russia, India and China) is diversifying or reversing the direction of these flows.

One of the most far-reaching effects of globalization is a weakening of the usual connection between a cultural event and its geographical location as a result of the dematerialization or deterritorialization processes facilitated by information and communication technologies. Indeed, globalization transports distant events, influences and experiences into our immediate vicinity, notably through visual and audio media. This weakening of the traditional ties between cultural experience and geographical location brings new influences and experiences into people's everyday lives. Digital cultures, for example, are having a considerable impact on cultural identities, especially among young people. In this way, an attitude of *cosmopolitanism* is developing, especially in the world's megalopolises. In some cases, this attenuation of ties to place may be experienced as a source of opportunity; in other cases, as a source of anxiety, loss of certainty and marginalization, leading on occasion to identity backlashes. Still, as our identities are inextricably bound to the environments in which we grew up and those in which we live, the effect does not generally amount to a radical break with our cultural background or to cultural homogenization.

International migration has become a significant factor in intercultural dynamics. In countries of emigration, the drain on human resources—tending among other things to skew the relationship between the sexes and generations—inevitably entails some weakening of the socio-cultural fabric. In the receiving countries, migrants face the challenge of reconciling a traditional system of values, cultural norms and social codes with the often very different customs of the host countries. Among the possible responses to this challenge, most immigrants avoid the extremes of complete assimilation or outright rejection in favour of a partial adaptation to their new cultural environment while preserving their ties with their cultures of origin, notably through family connections or the media. The influx of sizeable numbers of migrant workers and the development of de facto multicultural communities prompts a complex range of responses, mirroring to some degree those of the immigrant population itself. The outcome of the implicit negotiations between these communities is usually some measure of pluralism, ranging from institutional recognition to tolerance of difference. In these circumstances, conviviality may put down roots if it is not thwarted by ideologies of exclusion. These roots may in turn nurture new cultural expressions, since diversity is always potentially in the making.

[…]

International tourism is another phenomenon with a potentially significant impact on cultural diversity. Its growth in recent decades is suggested by comparing the number of international tourists in 1950, estimated at 25.3 million, with the 800 million recorded tourists in 2005 and the World Tourism Organization's forecast of a global tourist flow of almost 1 billion in 2010. A significant trend has been the increase in tourism to the developing world, reflected in the average annual growth in tourist arrivals in the Middle East (9 percent), East Africa and the Pacific (7 percent) and Africa (5 percent). The qualitative—as distinct from the *quantitative*—impact of this increase in the volume of intercultural contacts is obviously difficult to gauge. On the one hand, international tourism is to some extent self-contained and can generate new sources of income for local populations within the tourism industry and positively contribute to greater knowledge and understanding of different cultural environments and practices. On the other hand, the sheer volume of exchanges, even if in large part functional and transitory, carries with it with the risk of culturally "freezing" local populations as objects of tourism. Such cultural fixity further marginalizes these populations "since it is their marginality that they exhibit and sell for profit" (Azarya, 2004). While the immediate prospects for tourism growth remain unpredictable, it seems clear that intercultural contacts, including substantive exchanges, will continue to grow as a result of increased—and increasingly multidirectional—tourist flows, both real and virtual.

Both Positive and Negative Impacts

Within a broader international context, the globalization of international exchanges is leading to the integration of a diversity of multicultural services and expressions in many countries. An obvious example is the expanding range of foreign restaurants found throughout the industrialized world, catering for immigrant and local populations alike. Reproduced in a wide variety of contexts, notably in the worlds of fashion and entertainment, this juxtaposition of cultural expressions and experiences is leading to a greater interaction and merging of cultural forms. Such examples, reflecting a more general intensification of transnational flows, are consistent with a trend towards multiple cultural affiliations and a "complexification" of cultural identities. These new and growing intercultural phenomena reflect the dynamic character of cultural diversity, which cannot be assimilated into fixed repertoires of cultural manifestations and is constantly assuming new forms within evolving cultural settings.

Yet such positive outcomes should not lead us to underestimate the negative impacts of globalizing trends on the diversity of cultural expressions and on those for whom these expressions are intrinsic to their ways of life and very being. What is at stake for them is existential loss, not simply the disappearance of manifestations of human diversity. UNESCO's action in safeguarding intangible cultural heritage has highlighted some of the threats to traditional cultural expressions posed by what many see as the juggernaut of globalization. The supporters of the Carnaval de Oruro in Bolivia, for example, complain of the "ill-conceived globalization trends that impose common rules and behaviour, disregarding cultural particularities" and the "neoliberal tendency to analyze human activities from a cost-benefit perspective, without considering the magical and spiritual aspects of the Carnaval." For the epic storytellers of Kyrgyzstan, it is the rise of the modern entertainment market that explains why the younger generations in their country are ceasing to identify with ancient cultural performances. These clashes between "tradition" and 'modernity' are ubiquitous and problematic in terms of how they are to be perceived and addressed.

Over the last decade, a wide range of threats to traditional cultural expressions have been brought to the attention of UNESCO as the United Nations agency mainly responsible for protection of the world's cultural heritage in its tangible and intangible expressions. They include:

- The development of sedentary lifestyles, reflected in increasing urbanization: this is the case, for example, with the indigenous Záparas people in Ecuador and Peru. In Morocco, the strong urbanizing tendencies in the Sahara have brought about a progressive disappearance of the nomadic lifestyle, together with whole segments of cultural life, such as traditional handicrafts and poetry.
- Religious intolerance: the defenders of Maya Achi identity in Guatemala stress the grave harm that can be done to their culture by the influence of fundamentalist Christian sects that view their traditional customs as pagan—if not "diabolic"—activities to be eliminated.
- Lack of respect for forms of knowledge transmission in certain traditional societies: thus, in Nigeria, the Isa see the introduction of free primary education in the west of the country, dating from 1955, as the reason for a growing lack of interest among younger generations in their culture, particularly since Christian and Islamic doctrines are taught in school to the exclusion of traditional African religions. In Vanuatu, the time young children spend at school and in school activities are said to have kept them from learning the traditional practice of sand drawing, which is in decline.
- The world culture relayed by the media: in India, defenders of the art of Kutiyattam say that they are unable to compete with the mass media, especially radio and television programmes. This complaint is echoed in China by the practitioners of the Guqin, a seven-string musical instrument related to the zither.
- Failure to respect the sacred or devotional character of certain ceremonies: this is emphasized by the defenders of the Mask Dance of the Drums from Drametse, who deplore

the growing lack of interest among the young generation in the deep spirituality of these practices.

- The "museification" of practices that were previously forms of collective leisure serving to preserve and strengthen social bonds, as in the case of the Opera dei Puppi in Sicily (Italy).

- The replacement of ancient forms of cultural expression by new communication technologies: thus portable telephones and e-mails in Jamaica have rendered virtually obsolete the traditional means of communication in the form of the drum and abeng (conch shell), undermining the ancient musical traditions.

- The impact of global distribution networks on local cinema productions: one example among many is French-speaking African cinema, which, following a splendid decade in the 1980s, has experienced a period of crisis mainly attributable to a decline in local demand; local viewers are influenced by foreign television and film as a result of the proliferation of parabolic antennae and low-cost access to recent films through DVDs.

To meet these threats to cultural diversity—to its expressions in word, sound, image, print and artistic works and activities—the international community adopted, in 2003, the UNESCO *Convention for the Safeguarding of the Intangible Cultural Heritage* and, in 2005, the UNESCO *Convention on the Protection and Promotion of the Diversity of Cultural Expressions.*

It would be a mistake, however, to see the effects of globalization on cultural diversity as wholly negative, if only because there is nothing inevitable about the general trend towards cultural homogenization. As Claude Lévi-Strauss (2007) noted in a recent communication to UNESCO: "Time does not always move in the same direction. Periods of pervasive uniformity can be followed by unexpected reversals. This has happened in the past, and there are grounds for hoping that at the heart of the globalization process itself new forms of diversity whose nature we do not suspect may be in gestation." The rapid growth of digital cultures, for example, has given rise to new forms of cultural diversity, particularly among the young. Computer-mediated interactions through Internet sites, such as YouTube, Teen Second Life, FaceBook or MySpace, are means whereby people today "live" increasingly in more than one reality. The innumerable possible combinations of the new media for cultural expressions and cultural practices creates a whole host of "do-it-yourself cultures," which open the way to a broad range of new forms of cultural diversity.

Rather than attempting to evaluate the overall effect of globalization, to draw up a balance sheet of the forms of diversity that are disappearing compared with those coming into existence, it is more important to focus on the dynamic character of cultural diversity and to devise approaches to better managing the impact of cultural change on our individual and collective identities. Such efforts must also be complemented by the awareness that we cannot hope to preserve everything that is threatened with disappearance. As Claude Lévi-Strauss has observed, it is "diversity itself which must be saved, not the outward and visible form in which each period has clothed that diversity." It is important, then, to envisage new strategies for revitalizing cultural expressions and practices while helping vulnerable populations to acquire the tools necessary to "manage" cultural change more effectively. A dynamic conception of this kind leads us to question a number of inoperative dichotomies and received categories, such as the opposition between tradition and modernity. Every living tradition is susceptible to continual reinvention, which makes it relevant to the present. Tradition is no more reducible to the past than is modernity to the present or future. For tradition, like memory or culture, is inscribed within a process of becoming. Cultural diversity, like cultural identity, is about innovation, creativity and receptiveness to new cultural forms and relationships.

[…]

Financial Globalization Can Lead to Increased Volatility

Jonathan D. Ostry

Jonathan D. Ostry currently serves as deputy director of the research department at the International Monetary Fund (IMF). He is also a research fellow at the Centre for Economic Policy Research (CEPR) and the author of numerous books on international economics.

Economists tend to be advocates of globalization. The benefits of specialization and exchange are evident within a country's borders: no one would seriously suggest that impeding the flows of goods, labour and capital within a country would raise national welfare. Globalization extends the possibilities of specialization beyond national boundaries. Recent work suggests, however, that while globalization is great in theory, vigilance is needed about it in practice.

The three main components of globalization—goods, labour, and capital—are associated with different costs and benefits. The preponderance of the evidence suggests that trade has positive impacts on aggregate incomes, but many people do lose out. The economic benefits of migration are very high, but it too has distributional consequences and impacts on social cohesion.

The case for globalization is weakest when it comes to free flows of capital across national boundaries ("financial globalization"). The growth benefits claimed for these policies have proven elusive. At the same time, they are associated with an increase in inequality. Hence they pose a dilemma for proponents of globalization.

There are also interactions between financial globalization and other policies. In particular, financial globalization binds the conduct of domestic fiscal policy and leads to greater consolidation, which also has distributional effects.

"To Save Globalization, Its Benefits Need to Be More Broadly Shared," by Jonathan D. Ostry, World Economic Forum, January 16, 2017. Reprinted by permission.

Aggregate and Distributional Effects of Financial Globalization

As many have argued, economic theory leaves no doubt about the potential advantages of capital account liberalization. It can allow the international capital market to channel world savings to their most productive uses across the globe. Developing countries with little capital can borrow to finance investment, thereby promoting their economic growth without requiring commensurate increases in their own saving. But equally, there is little doubt about the existence of genuine hazards of openness to foreign financial flows. This duality of benefits and risks is simply a fact of life in the real world.

The experience of countries with financial opening/openness bears this out. As Ostry and others (2009) and many subsequent studies have shown, the link between financial globalization and economic growth turns out to be complex. While some capital flows such as foreign direct investment boost long-run growth, the impact of other flows is weaker and critically dependent on a country's other institutions (the quality of its legal framework; protection of property rights; level of financial development; quality of financial supervision) and how openness is sequenced relative to other policy changes.

Moreover, openness to capital flows has tended to increase economic volatility and the frequency of crises in many emerging markets and developing economies. As a recent study has shown, about 20% of the time, surges end in a financial crisis, of which one-half are also associated with large output declines—what one might call a growth crisis. The ubiquity of surges and crashes gives credence to the claim by Harvard economist Dani Rodrik that "boom-and-bust cycles are hardly a sideshow or a minor blemish in international capital flows; they are the main story."

Capital Surges and Financial Crises

While the drivers of surges and crashes are many, increased capital account openness consistently figures as a risk factor—it raises the probability of a surge and of a post-surge crash. In addition to raising the odds of a crash, openness has distributional effects, raising inequality, especially when a crash ensues.

Financial globalization also interacts with other policies, notably fiscal policy. The desire to attract foreign capital can trigger a "race to the bottom" in effective corporate tax rates, lowering governments' ability to provide essential public goods. Fiscal consolidation has been shown to increase inequality.

Such direct and indirect distributional effects could set up an adverse feedback loop: the increase in inequality might itself undercut growth, which is what globalization is intent on increasing in the first place. There is now strong evidence that inequality lowers both the level and the durability of growth. Hence, the existence of such a loop is not a theoretical curiosum but a very real possibility.

The Way Forward

These findings suggest several steps to re-design globalization. The first step is to recognize the flaws in globalization, especially in relation to financial globalization. The adverse effects of financial globalization on macroeconomic volatility and inequality should be countered. Among policymakers today, there is increased acceptance of capital controls to restrict foreign capital flows that are viewed as likely to lead to—or compound—a financial crisis. While not the only tools available, capital controls may be the best option when it is borrowing from abroad that is the source of an unsustainable credit boom.

Beyond this, *in the short run*, the extent of redistribution could be increased. This can be done through some combination of increases in tax rates (greater progressivity in income taxes; increased reliance on wealth and property taxes) and programs to help those who lose out from globalization.

- In the case of trade, programs of adjustment assistance do exist. That such programs have not always worked well in the past is an argument for fixing them, not for discarding them. "Trampoline" policies—including job retraining and assistance with search—to help workers bounce back from job displacement are essential.

- In the case of migration too, compensation to potential losers could be expanded by targeting areas of high entry of foreign workers. This can be done through more generous unemployment insurance benefits and greater resources devoted to active labor market policies to match displaced workers to jobs.

In the longer run, the solutions lie not in redistribution but in mechanisms that achieve "pre-distribution." More equal access to health, education, and financial services ensures that market incomes are not simply a function of peoples' starting point in life. This does not ensure that everyone will end up at the same point. But the provision of opportunities to do well in life regardless of initial income level, combined with the promise of redistribution for those who fall behind, is more likely to build support for globalization than will simply ignoring the discontent with it.

Globalization's Negative Impacts on Mental Health Among People from Non-Western Cultures

Narayan Gopalkrishnan

Narayan Gopalkrishnan is the Course Coordinator of Social Work at James Cook University in Australia. He is a research fellow with the Cairns Institute.

Culture is a broad and vexed term that can be defined in a range of ways, depending on the field of study and the perspective of the person using the term. As [Rachel] Tribe argues, it is a multi-layered concept influenced by a range of issues such as gender, class, religion, language, and nationality, just to name a few. [Anthony] Giddens, from a sociological perspective, presents culture as the set of values that the members of a given group hold and includes the norms they follow and the material goods that they create. For the purposes of this paper we are using the term in the context of ethnic identity, or the multidimensional set of ascriptive group identities to which religion, language, and race (as a social construct) belong and all of which contribute to a person's view of themselves.

Culture, in itself, is impacted on by the broader context of social norms and social issues. For example, many refugees, and migrants in Western countries work at the lower ends of the labor market, with lower pay and higher levels of casualization than the general population. As such they experience much higher levels of income inequality within these countries, inequalities that in turn impact adversely on their health and wellbeing. While acknowledging the key impacts of these larger social issues, and recognizing the need for broad and collective responses to their impacts on cultural

Narayan Gopalkrishnan, "Cultural Diversity and Mental Health: Considerations for Policy and Practice," *Frontiers in Public Health*, June 19, 2018. https://www.frontiersin.org/articles/10.3389/fpubh.2018.00179/full. Licensed under CC BY 4.0 International.

groups, this paper will focus on the impacts that culture has on mental health so as to excavate the key considerations for policy and practice within this context.

Much of the theory and practice of mental health, including psychiatry and mainstream psychology, have emerged from Western cultural traditions and Western understandings of the human condition. Notions of Cartesian dualism of body and mind, positivism, and reductionism have been central to the development of mainstream mental health systems as they are widely implemented today. While these relatively monocultural understandings of mental health have provided powerful conceptual tools and frameworks for the alleviation of mental distress in many settings, they have also been very problematic when applied to the context of non-Western cultures without consideration of the complexity that working across cultures brings with it. Tribe suggests that Western cultural approaches to health tend to be "predicated on a model that focuses on individual intrapsychic experience or individual pathology, while other traditions may be based more on community or familial processes." From issues of over-representation of particular cultural groups in mental health facilities to research that excludes cultural groups and includes others, there are a number of areas at the intersection of mental health and culture that need to be considered by the mental health professional if they wish to effectively engage with all of the people that they work with.

Cultural diversity across the world has significant impacts on the many aspects of mental health, ranging from the ways in which health and illness are perceived, health seeking behavior, attitudes of the consumer as well as the practitioners and mental health systems. As [Mario] Hernandez et al. suggest "culture influences what gets defined as a problem, how the problem is understood and which solutions to the problem are acceptable." Many of these considerations in cultural diversity and mental health will be explored in the rest of the paper, an exploration of importance in that while it may point to areas that need to be strengthened, it will also point to opportunities that exist where new forms of engagement could be explored and the needs of people of diverse cultures could be met more effectively and sustainably.

Key Considerations

[Regina] Hechanova and [Lynn]Waeldle suggest that there are five key components of diverse cultures that have implications for mental health professionals. While the authors make their arguments in the specific context of disaster situations in Southeast Asia, their comments provide a framework to begin the discussion of cultural diversity and mental health. The first element that they identify is *emotional expression* where some cultures may identify that lack of balance in expression may lead to disease. Further, this may be reflected in a perception that talking about painful issues would lead to further painful feelings. This reluctance to utilize talking therapies is evidenced in other research especially with refugees from Africa and from Southeast Asia. The second element is *shame* which Hechanova and Waelde argue is one of the reasons why Asians are slow to access professional therapists. Shame may play a key part in this context because of the significant role that family plays in the lives of Asian individuals with mental health issues. The third element that they discuss is *power distance* or the large differences in power that may exist in Asian countries between therapist and which may have implications in terms of the autonomy or lack thereof in the therapeutic relationship. Fourth they discuss the nature of *collectivism* and its impact as a supportive factor to resilience and coping. And finally, they discuss *spirituality and religion* from the point of view of attribution as well as in terms of coping with disease. These five factors are useful to further excavate some of the considerations that we explore in this section.

There is an extensive body of research literature that emphasizes the fact that health and illness are perceived differently across cultures. Cultural meanings of health and illness have "real consequences in terms of whether people are motivated to seek treatment, how they cope with their symptoms, how supportive their families and communities are, where they seek help (mental health specialist, primary care provider, clergy, and/or traditional healer), the pathways they take to get services, and how well they fare in treatment." To begin with, the *perceptions of* etiology of disease can be very different across cultures. [Cecil] Helman presents us with a framework of views of illness causality that may be at the individual level or situated in the natural world or in the social world, and argues that each cultural group views these differently. Some cultures may ascribe the onset of disease to possession by spirits, the "evil eye," black magic or the breaking of taboos, which then places the rectification of the problem within the purview of traditional healers, elders, or other significant people in the community. Religion and spirituality play a key part in these perceptions by juxtaposing hardship with a higher order good and the solutions are accordingly sought within the purview of these systems. Examples of these would be the healing temples in India or other religious pilgrimage sites across the world that are visited every day by thousands of people experiencing mental health issues.

Diverse views in terms of etiology are also central to the large traditional health systems in countries like India and China. For example, the disease factors in Traditional Chinese Medicine are often ascribed to a lack of balance between pathogenic factors of Yin and Yang. In Ayurveda, the major traditional healing system in India, mental health may be perceived to be a product of karma or one's actions, vayu or air, and swabhave or one's nature. An important factor in both these healing systems is that the demarcation between body and mind is not emphasized, and the patient is treated as a whole, and in the context of his/her external environment. It is important to note that people from diverse cultures may not make the same distinction between issues of the body and the mind as in Western therapeutic systems. In their research with Afghan refugees in the Netherlands, [Titia] Feldmann et al. found that the participants made no distinction between mental and physical health. This is very unlike Western biomedicine, which has traditionally taken a reductionist approach that clearly separates the body and the mind. Research in more recent times clearly points to the interrelationship between body and mind, and areas of study such as psychosomatic medicine and psychoneuroimmunology have provided substantial evidence that methods working with a composite of the body and mind in the context of the environment are more likely to be effective than dualistic and reductionist approaches. In the context of cultures that are already familiar with these integrative approaches, we would argue that there is potential for new approaches to working with distress, whether of the body or the mind.

Cultures vary also in terms of how they *seek treatment* from mainstream Western health system. [Jihlam] Biswas et al. argue that those seeking help from mainstream health systems in India tended to present more often with somatic symptoms whereas those in the United States tended to present more with cognitive based symptoms. Further, research in High Income Countries (HICs) like Australia, Canada and the United States emphasizes that diverse cultures in these countries tend to seek help much later than those from the majority community and many of them tend to present in acute stages of mental distress. One of the reasons for this can be the nature of shame as discussed in some of the research with migrants and refugees in HICs as well as with general populations in Low and Middle-Income Countries (LMICs) in Asia and Southeast Asia. [Nan Zhang] Hampton and [Seneca E.] Sharp have explored the nature of shame quite comprehensively using a framework of external, internal and reflective shame to argue that mental health systems, professionals, and researchers need to recognize and mediate the effects of shame on individuals from diverse cultures if they wish to ensure effective management of mental health issues. Hechanova and Waedle suggest that shame related reasons for low access to mental health systems could be due to several reasons. The first possibility is about the desire to protect the family reputation and their own dignity. The second relates to the possibility that the mental health professional would see them as "crazy," similar to the notion of external shame, and finally that the person may be reluctant to open up to strangers, due to a number of factors such as fears of "loss of face," lack of trust, or the fear of revisiting painful events. Research indicates that talking therapies may not be the most useful form of intervention among many cultural groups. The National Child Traumatic Stress Network in the United States argues that "talking about painful events may not be experienced as valuable or therapeutic by refugees from societies where psychological models are not hegemonic." This perception of talking therapies in turn raises the possibilities of more effective utilization of movement-based therapies, expressive therapies, online therapies.

Stigma can play a key role in terms of variations in treatment-seeking. Stigma can be viewed as a "mark of shame, disgrace or disapproval which results in an individual being rejected, discriminated against, and excluded from participating in a number of different areas of society." Stigma around depression and other mental illness can be higher in some cultural groups and often is a major barrier to people from diverse cultures when accessing mental health services. Stigma can cause people to feel so ashamed that they hide their symptoms and do not seek treatment until the issues becomes acute. Stigma can be examined from a range of related issues such as the perceptions of etiology as well as notions of shame and levels of interdependence in the community. In the context of Low and Medium Income Countries, these issues become even more significant as the family is often the only safety net that individuals have. Where government safety nets are minimal or do not exist, lack of support from the family due to perceptions of stigma can lead to total neglect of a person with mental health issues.

[…]

Racism and discrimination impact quite dramatically on many diverse cultural groups. While older forms of racism were ideologies that supported the notion of biological "races" and ranked them in terms of superior and inferior, these have since been superseded by newer forms of racism that are built on more complex notions of cultural superiority or inferiority. Besides the negative attitudes and beliefs that are implicit in all forms of racism, they also lead to discrimination and differential treatment of individuals of some cultural groups. The experience of racism can lead to social alienation of the individual, a fear of public spaces, loss of access to services, and a range of other effects that in turn impact adversely on the mental health of the affected individual. [David R.] Williams and [Selina A.] Mohammed, based on their systematic literature review, argue that "the consistency of an inverse association between discrimination for an increasingly broad range of health outcomes, across multiple population groups in a wide range of cultural and national contexts is impressive, and lends credibility to the plausibility of perceived discrimination as an important emerging risk factor for disease." In the present hostile environment to Muslims in many HICs, women who dress in a way that identifies them clearly with Islam can especially bear a significant amount of individual and institutionalized racism and discrimination, with significant impacts on their mental health. Discrimination is also one of the major barriers to Aboriginal Peoples accessing mental health services, especially when the service is within a non-Aboriginal mental health setting.

As part of the discussion of racism and discrimination, notions of mainstream bias and the stereotyping of cultural groups in healthcare need consideration. The history of working with diverse cultural groups in healthcare in High Income Countries has numerous examples of stereotyping of specific cultural groups leading to interventions that are often inadequate or inappropriate. The very concepts of normality and abnormality in Western therapeutic approaches are embedded in cultural constructions that cannot be easily generalized across cultures. These can lead to situations where "health practitioners overlook, misinterpret, stereotype, or otherwise mishandle their encounters with those who might be viewed as different from them in their assessment, intervention, and evaluation-planning processes." Of particular concern here is the overdiagnosis of particular cultural groups with particular mental disorders as in the case of the overdiagnosis of schizophrenia in African American communities.

Coping and resilience are other areas of consideration in the context of cultural diversity and mental health. Coping styles refer to the ways in which people cope with both everyday as well and more extreme stressors in their lives, including mental health related stressors. The US Surgeon General posits that a better understanding of the ways diverse cultural groups cope with adversity has "implications for the promotion of mental health, the prevention of mental illness, and the nature and severity of mental health problems." Aldwin suggests that cultural groups can show major differences in terms of the types of stressors that they experience, and how they assess these stressors. Different cultures may place stressful events differently as normative, or something that most people in that culture will experience, such as coming-of-age rituals. Further they will allocate social resources differently, leading to diverse experiences of these stressors. And finally, they may assess stressors differently, such as in terms of breaking of taboos or other cultural norms. This diversity in terms of dealing with stressors can be both a protective factor and a risk factor. Hechanova and Waelde suggest that, in collectivist cultures, healing is a product of interdependence and that the health of the group is at least as important to the individual as his or her own health.

Closely associated with coping, resilience is the ability to do well despite facing adversity, and is often discussed in the context of traits and characteristics of individuals. [Laurence J.] Kirmayer et al. argue that the psychological approaches to resilience have emphasized individual traits rather than the systemic or ecological roots of resilience. They go on to suggest that, in the context of the Aboriginal Peoples of Canada, resilience is embedded in cultural values, renewed cultural identity, revitalized collective history, language, culture, spirituality, healing, and collective action. As discussed earlier, collectivist cultures can play a key role as both a protective factor and a risk factor in issues of mental health.

In many cultural groups, *the family* can be very involved in all aspects of a person's life. Family factors such as supportive extended families and strong sibling relationships can act as protective factors in mental health, while perceptions of stigma, severe marital discord, breaking of norms and other such factors can be major risk factors. Which would suggest that interventions that include cultural renewal and community and family support systems can be very useful in some or most cultural groups.

Cultural impacts on the therapeutic relationship are a significant factor to be considered in working with diverse cultures in mental health. The cultural context of the client and the practitioner are both central to the therapeutic relationship, a relationship that cannot work without careful consideration of the implications of cultural diversity. Ideally, both the therapist and the client would be from the same culture and some of the pitfalls can be avoided. However, even in these circumstances, the practitioner brings their own "professional" culture with them which can create a cultural gap with the client. In practice, there is a strong likelihood that therapists would be working with clients from cultures very different from their own and making assessments without linguistic, conceptual and normative equivalence, which could lead to many errors in service provision decision. Some of the issues of overdiagnosis of certain cultural groups with particular mental disorders as mentioned earlier may find its roots with this lack of equivalence in assessment. Still further considerations involve the concept of *culture as language.* Language is central to any culture and to cultural understanding, and yet in HICs such as Australia the therapist and the client may not even share the same language. While many High Income Countries have policies in place to ensure that appropriate interpreters are used in such circumstances, an endemic problem of non-utilization of interpreters continues.

Society as a patient is a term that [Anthony J.] Marsella uses to point out that not all problems are located within the individual, and that the patient's well-being or lack thereof is often a product of the impacts of the external environment. This is particularly the case with migrants and refugees or Indigenous populations in HICs who may experience racism, discrimination, and attendant marginalization. Marsella goes on to argue for mental health professionals who work across cultures to take up the roles of social activists and challenge some of the societal contexts that are impacting on their clients (2011). This societal context also involves globalization and the rapid change of systems and cultures. Globalization is not a new process but the last 100 years has seen a rapid increase in global networks, increased velocity of global flows and increased depth of global interconnectedness. Culture has been impacted by these global flows with the increasing domination of notions of individualism, materialism, and social fragmentation, and where "well-being may be a collateral casualty of the economic, social and cultural changes associated with globalization." The loss of social networks as protective factors can be very significant in terms of increasing levels of distress in culturally diverse communities such as refugees and migrants in HICs. Traditional healers and healing systems are being replaced by Western systems that can suffer from inadequate resourcing and may be culturally inappropriate. All of which points to the need for ways forward that build on these diminishing resources and strengthen the capacity of individuals and communities toward better mental health outcomes. Some possible future directions are discussed in the next section.

Ways Forward

Mainstream mental health systems are increasingly acknowledging the intersection of cultural diversity. As an example, the provision of the *cultural formulation interview* in the DSM-5 is a positive step especially as it seeks to explore cultural identity, conceptualization of illness, psychosocial stressors, vulnerability, and resilience as well as the cultural features of the relationship between the clinician and the patient. However, this is just one tool in the larger picture and cannot mean anything without more radical changes in systems and practices. Much of the literature in the field points to the need for holistic health services that incorporate the total context in which health and illness are experienced. Some suggestions involve the integration of mental health services with primary health care as a way of getting past some of the stigma and discrimination issues. As [Chee] Ng et al. posit in the context of Low and Medium Income Countries "integrating mental health services into primary health care is a highly practical and viable way of closing the mental health treatment gap in settings where there are resource constraints." Which is not to say that the same does not apply to the High-Income Countries like Australia where effective mental health responses in many Indigenous communities continue to be an unmet goal. More recent approaches such as the *biopsychosocial* and the *recovery* approaches in mental health or renewed calls for *medical pluralism* also offer new opportunities to work with people in a more holistic way.

[Suman] Fernando suggests that "[m]ental health development, like development in any other field, must start by tapping into what people in any location currently want and value." One of the ways that needs to exploration more systematically is the possibility of integrating *positive resources in the community* into the provision of mental health services. Marsella argues that community-based ethno-cultural services are a positive resource in the community that can provide an essential function in working with mental health issues in diverse cultural groups. Further, he argues that the development of a strong social support and community-based network must be intrinsic to the process. In the context of working with refugees in the UK, Tribe also endorses this view, suggesting that community-based mental health services "may prove more accessible, acceptable and relevant services which are more in line with other types of community care." Besides these forms of services, there is also significant evidence to show that many people within culturally diverse communities are likely to utilize avenues other than professional therapists for dealing with mental distress, such elders in the community, religious leaders, priests, and traditional healers. These positive resources, including especially *traditional healing practices and systems* can be involved in the provision of mental health services through collaborations, partnerships, and community-based health systems. An example here is the Muthuswamy healing temple in India where research conducted by the National Institute of Mental Health and Neurological Sciences (NIMHANS), India concluded that people with mental health issues staying at the temple showed significant reduction in psychiatric rating scale scores. The researchers suggested that "[h]ealing temples may constitute a community resource for mentally ill people in cultures where they are recognized and valued ... [and the] potential for effective alliances involving indigenous local resources needs to be considered." Similarly, [Joseph P.] Gone points to the widespread use of talking circles, pipe ceremonies, sweat lodges and other culturally specific practices in the federal Indian Health Service in the United States to argue for a renewed focus on participation in traditional cultural practices, and attendant possibilities of spiritual transformations, shifts in collective identity and meaning making. [Patricia] Boksa et al. also reiterate the centrality of local Indigenous knowledge as a guide to the development of relevant mental health systems. [Joyce Maureen] Mahony and [Tom Truong] Donnelly also point out that spiritual and traditional healing practices can prove very useful in terms of promoting immigrant women's mental health.

Another way forward is to go beyond *cultural competence* frameworks and practice toward developing *cultural partnerships.* Cultural competence "refers to the awareness, knowledge, and skills and the processes needed by individuals, profession, organizations and systems to function effectively and appropriately in culturally diverse situations in general and in particular encounters from different cultures." Quite a few authors point to cultural competence as the most commonly used framework of practice in working with issues of mental health in culturally diverse settings. While the cultural competence framework has proved useful in terms of working across cultures, it suffers from a few significant flaws. Firstly, cultural competence frameworks approach culture from a purportedly value-neutral position, thereby ignoring the differences in power and the nature of historical and present-day oppression experienced by cultural groups. Secondly the "competence" approach focuses on the providers and their institutions and their capabilities to provide culturally appropriate services and disregards the participation of the clients and their communities. In circumstances where some cultural groups can be marginalized, as in the context of the issues of historical dispossession, racism, stereotyping, stigmatization, and power differentials, it becomes extremely important to work toward more equitable ways of engaging with communities. And finally, cultural competence draws on static notions of cultures that are not based on the reality of the constantly changing and transforming nature of cultures.

These issues point toward the need for developing partnerships that are more equitable and that realign power relationships between service providers and individuals. The focus must be to move from traditional relationships built in power relationships to more interdependent and synergistic relationships. A range of partnerships could be useful toward developing more effective mental health systems. They could include cultural partnerships between mental health providers and diverse cultural communities. It would certainly add to the nature of these partnerships if the providers also followed a deliberate policy of hiring workers of diverse backgrounds, and especially those from the communities that the service users come from. [Sally B.] Murray and [Susan A.] Skull suggest that these forms of partnerships between refugee groups and health service providers have been shown to be more effective in terms of responding to health and other needs of the refugees than traditional top-down approaches. Partnerships could also be developed between mental health providers and traditional healers and/or community elders where synergies could be built on. Finally, the relationship between the therapist and the client could be viewed as a cultural partnership, very much in line with the recovery approach, where the client would be an active participant in the process.

Conclusion

In this article, some of the key considerations of working with diverse cultures in mental health have been explored and the point made that there can be severe repercussions on individuals and communities if systems and processes are not in place to enable mental health providers to work effectively across cultures. Each of these considerations in turn provides opportunities for new ways of engaging across cultures that can empower all parties involved rather than disempower and marginalize some groups while empowering others. Rather than approach the considerations from a deficit approach, where each of these is a problem, they can provide new avenues for developing integrated and holistic approaches toward working with mental health. A few of these avenues have been discussed in the paper, and some of these are already beginning to make inroads into mainstream mental health services, such as the emphasis on integrative services and the recovery approach. Others, which have been delineated in greater detail in this paper, such as working with positive resources in the community and cultural partnerships, are those where very small one-off projects have been embarked on and where arguably there is much more opportunity for broad based research and practice.

Trade Policy and the Economic Health of the United States

The World Trade Organization

The World Trade Organization (WTO) is an international organization dedicated to promoting free trade and economic development. The WTO provides a venue for negotiating trade agreements and works to promote economic cooperation and productive dialogue between countries.

The United States continues to be the world's largest trading nation in exports and imports of goods and services. Over the past decade, trade has become increasingly important for the US economy with the ratio of trade to GDP in 1995 reaching 23.6 per cent, up from 17.2 per cent in 1985 and 20.6 per cent in 1990. A new WTO Secretariat report on the trade policies and practices of the United States notes that the US invests less as a share of GDP than its industrial counterparts but with very efficient resource allocation, capital productivity is high, a factor that underpins US prosperity. The report stresses the need to keep markets securely open as a major element in maintaining US productivity growth.

The report confirms that WTO commitments are at the centre of US trade policy. The application of the Uruguay Round Agreements and the consolidation of trade remedy measures under WTO dispute settlement procedures have stabilized many elements in US trade policy that at times were perceived by some as unpredictable and unilateralist. In parallel to the implementation of its WTO commitments, the United States has continued with regional, bilateral and unilateral trade initiatives. The report observes that the US' multi-track approach to international trade policy can be a source of tension within the multilateral system. The WTO report and a policy statement by the Government of the

"United States: October 1996," World Trade Organization, October 31, 1996. Reprinted by permission. © 1996 WTO.

United States, will be the subject of two days of discussion at the WTO's Trade Policy Review Body on 11 and 12 November 1996.

[…]

The report discusses changes in US anti-dumping and countervailing legislation, and notes that it is too early to assess whether these changes will facilitate affirmative findings. The number of anti-dumping and countervailing investigations launched in the US has dropped sharply, perhaps due to the continuing US economic recovery. Three safeguard investigations were conducted in 1995 and 1996 with one investigation concluding that imports caused injury to the domestic industry.

The use of "Section 301" legislation is now closely tied to multilateral dispute settlement, at least for WTO members and in areas subject to WTO rules and disciplines. The United States is the most active user of WTO dispute settlement provisions; it has requested consultations under WTO dispute settlement provisions on 19 cases covering 17 measures, while US trading partners have raised nine complaints against eight US measures. Since its last trade policy review in 1994, the US has initiated 16 "301" investigations and concluded agreements covering two previous investigations. Seven of the 301 actions initiated in 1996 and two earlier investigations (European Union, bananas; and Japan, photographic film and paper) have been referred to the WTO Dispute Settlement Body.

In separate developments, the US has enacted the Cuban Liberty and Democratic Solidarity (LIBERTAD) Act and the Iran and Libya Sanctions Act. The extra-territorial aspects of these laws have been criticised by US trading partners and cases against the LIBERTAD Act (Helms-Burton Act) have been filed under the North-American Free Trade Agreement (NAFTA) and the WTO.

Voluntary export restrictions administered by US trading partners have been phased out. A new automotive agreement with Japan does not set quantitative targets for US exports but provides for bilateral monitoring of various qualitative commitments, while a Memorandum of Understanding, which seeks to liberalize access to the Korean vehicle market, is to be implemented on an m.f.n. basis. A new co-operation agreement with Japan on semi-conductors reaffirms market principles and establishes a consultative framework open to industry associations whose governments are committed to tariff elimination.

The report notes that the US' technical regulations are generally based on international norms and privately developed standards; however, there are a limited number of mandatory environmental process standards enforced at the border, notable examples being "dolphin-friendly" tuna fishing methods and turtle-excluder devices used in harvesting shrimp.

The US has a well developed and enforced system of intellectual property protection based on constitutional provisions. The TRIPS Agreement increased the duration of protection and resurrected protection for works that had fallen into the US public domain. The report states that the United States monitors bilaterally the protection for intellectual property extended by all its trading partners, irrespective of whether a bilateral agreement is in force, the US is required to identify countries that deny adequate and effective protection for intellectual property rights or fair and equitable market access to US persons that rely on intellectual property protection.

The report notes that textile and clothing production has realized significant productivity gains on the basis of greater capital intensity in the US market and outward processing operations in Mexico, the Caribbean and Central America. In addition to import tariffs well above the manufacturing average, the United States maintains country specific import quotas under the WTO Agreement on Textiles and Clothing and has issued 25 safeguard quota calls on WTO members. Removal of import quotas is to be conducted in four phases and the allocation of all textile and clothing products to each phase has been published. The most sensitive products have been left to the last phase, to be implemented in 2005. The report also notes significant changes which have been made in the rules of origin used for the administration of import quotas. The origin of a product is now specified to be the place where it is assembled and not the place where the textile components are cut.

The WTO report notes that services have gained an increasing share of US output, generating about two-thirds of GDP, or some four times the share of manufacturing, and accounting for 65 per cent of employment in 1995. Cross-border supply of foreign services has become less important than establishment as a mode of delivery. While Western Europe is the US' largest trading partner for cross-border trade in services with approximately 60 per cent, Japan is the largest individual destination, taking in 15.5 per cent of US services exports. The report notes that productivity increases in services are likely to be a decisive factor in raising total US productivity growth and standards of living. Recent developments in the telecommunications, financial and professional services sectors have enhanced such prospects. The benefits to the United States of maintaining and improving on an efficient, open and competitive services sector are thus evident.

The report concludes that while an open, predictable world trading system is crucial for the well-being of the US economy, an open, predictable US market is also vital for the world's trading system. It is, therefore, essential that the United States and its partners utilize the system to maintain multilateralism as the key to future developments and discourage pressures for increased bilateralism or unilateralism.

[…]

The Secretariat's Report: Summary
The United States in World Trade
The US economy has performed well since the last Trade Policy Review of the United States. Growth has been above the average in industrial countries, inflation has remained moderate and the unemployment rate is at a low for the decade. Concurrently, the federal budget deficit has narrowed substantially, to its lowest share of gross domestic product since 1979. The external current account

deficit has widened slightly but this is attributable to increased investment, improving the prospects for future growth.

The US economy has a high degree of allocative efficiency. It invests less, as a share of output, than its industrial counterparts but capital productivity is well above the OECD average, a factor that underpins US prosperity. One important element in maintaining productivity is the openness of the US economy, which helps to keep economic actors under constant pressure to allocate resources efficiently. This also means that it is in the United States' own best interest to keep its markets securely open.

Trade has become increasingly important in US economic activity. The ratio of US trade to GDP has risen from 17.2 per cent in 1985, to 20.6 per cent in 1990 and to 23.6 per cent in 1995. This increased involvement in trade tends to serve as a counter-cyclical buffer. In the early 1990s, exports cushioned the impact of the US recession, demonstrating the importance for the United States that its producers have secure, liberal access to foreign markets, within a strong, rules-based multilateral system. Subsequently, as US growth improved, net imports accommodated excess domestic demand, allowing lower inflation, and interest rates, than might otherwise have been the case.

Since the last Review, the services sector has assumed an increasing share of US output. In part, this reflects differential inflation rates in the goods and services sectors, with higher rates in the latter; in recent years, productivity growth in manufacturing has exceeded that of GDP. However, with services accounting for about two-thirds of GDP, or some four times the share of manufacturing, it is clear that productivity growth in services is a determining factor in US living standards. The benefits to the United States of maintaining and improving on an efficient, open and competitive services sector are thus evident. This is especially the case for "input" services such as finance, communications and transport, where productivity gains can significantly lower costs in other sectors, such as manufacturing. Within this framework, it is also noteworthy that the cross-border supply of foreign services to the United States is now less important than establishment as a mode of delivery, emphasizing the ongoing interest of the United States in maintaining a liberal foreign direct investment régime.

The United States continues to be the world's largest single trading nation in goods and services, with some 15 per cent of merchandise and 16 per cent of services exports. The European Union remains the largest market for US merchandise exports but there is an ongoing shift in the direction of US trade toward east Asia, which is now the most important source of imports. The composition of US merchandise trade has also continued to move from primary toward manufactured products, in spite of rapidly growing agricultural exports. Growth of manufacturing exports has been broad-based, with increased shares for exports of office machines, telecommunications equipment, chemicals, iron and steel products and automotive products. The share of manufactures in merchandise imports has also increased, led by office machines and telecommunications equipment, non-electrical machinery, and chemicals; the share of automotive products has declined.

US markets and sources for goods and for services are, in general, closely correlated. While Western Europe as a group is the US largest trading partner for cross-border trade in services, accounting for approximately 60 per cent of imports and exports, Japan is the largest individual destination, with 15.5 per cent of US services exports. Transportation is the largest component of services exports, with over 50 per cent; however, exports of business services, royalties and licensing fees have grown rapidly, respectively doubling and increasing by 63 per cent during 1994–1995.

[…]

Outlook

While an open, predictable world trading system continues to be crucial for the well-being of the US economy, the converse is also true; an open, predictable US economy is crucial for the health of the world trading system. During the past two years, the US application of the Uruguay Round Agreements and the consolidation of trade remedy measures under WTO dispute settlement procedures have stabilized many elements that previously appeared unpredictable and unilateralist in US policy; the Administration has also showed restraint in using the instruments available and has accepted WTO rulings. However, elements of US trade legislation, even under the WTO, continue to cause concern for certain trading partners. Thus, the backloading of textile and clothing liberalization remains problematic for many developing countries, even though conditions of access have improved; access to government procurement remains restricted in various areas; and although the right to file suit under the Cuban Liberty and Democratic Solidarity (LIBERTAD) Act of 1996 has been deferred and, so far, no sanctions have been announced against companies investing in Iran or Libya, the extraterritorial application of US trade laws has attracted significant attention.

The United States continues to use three main tracks in its trade policy making: multilateral agreements concluded on a m.f.n. basis (as in the Uruguay Round); regional agreements; and unilateral pressure to open third-country markets (with bilateral resulting agreements normally applied on an m.f.n. basis). In some ongoing areas of multilateral negotiations, concerns about the lack of "adequate" reciprocity by some partners have governed US actions. While there is no doubt that US trade policy is firmly founded in the WTO system, the interaction among these various tracks remains a source of tension within the system. It is therefore crucial that the United States and its partners utilize the system to maintain multilateralism as the key to future developments and discourage pressures for increased bilateralism or unilateralism.

[...]

Critics Often Exaggerate the Scale and Depth of Globalization

Pankaj Ghemawat

Pankaj Ghemawat is a professor of management and strategy at New York University's Stern School of Business, where he also serves as director of the Center for Globalization Education and Management. He is also the lead author of the DHL Global Connectedness Index.

Business leaders are scrambling to adjust to a world few imagined possible just a year ago. The myth of a borderless world has come crashing down. Traditional pillars of open markets—the United States and the UK arc wobbling, and China is positioning itself as globalization's staunchest defender. In June 2016, the Brexit vote stunned the European Union, and the news coverage about globalization turned increasingly negative in the US as the presidential election campaign progressed.

One week after Donald Trump's inauguration, with fears of a trade war spiking, the *Economist* published a cover story, "The Retreat of the Global Company," in which it proclaimed that "the biggest business idea of the past three decades is in deep trouble" and that "the advantages of scale and … arbitrage have worn away." And Jeffrey Immelt, GE's chairman and CEO, has talked about the company's "bold pivot" from globalization to localization.

But is a mass retreat from globalization really the right approach for companies in these uncertain times? Or, short of packing up and returning home, should they focus on localization—that is, producing and even innovating where they sell—as the strategy of choice? Not according to my research. Recall that as recently as a decade ago, business leaders believed that the world was becoming "flat" and that global companies, unconstrained by country borders, would soon dominate the world economy. Those exaggerated

"Globalization in the Age of Trump," by Pankaj Ghemawat, Harvard Business School Publishing, July-August 2017. Reprinted by permission.

claims were proven wrong. Today's cries for a massive pullback from globalization in the face of new protectionist pressures are also an overreaction, in the other direction. While some of the euphoria about globalization has shifted to gloom, especially in the United States, globalization has yet to experience a serious reversal. And even if it did, it would be a mistake to talk about the end of globalization: The "rewind" button on a tape recorder shouldn't be confused with the "off" button.

A full-scale retreat or an overreliance on localization would hamper companies' ability to create value across borders and distance using the rich array of globalization strategies that are still effective—and will continue to work well into the future. Today's turmoil calls for a more subtle reworking of multinationals' strategies, organizational structures, and approaches to societal engagement. In this article, I address common misperceptions about what is—and isn't—changing about globalization, offer guidelines to help leaders decide where and how to compete, and examine multinationals' role in a complex world.

The Trajectory of Globalization

Doubts about the future of globalization began to surface during the 2008–2009 financial crisis. But as macroeconomic conditions improved, the gloom gave way to a murky mix of perspectives. For example, within the span of just three weeks in 2015, the *Washington Post* published an article by Robert J. Samuelson titled "Globalization at Warp Speed" and a piece from the editorial board called "The End of Globalization?"

In the face of such ambiguity, it is essential to look at the data. To see how globalization is actually evolving, Steven Altman and I compile the biennial DHL Global Connectedness Index, which tracks international flows of trade, capital, information, and people. The two index components of greatest business interest—merchandise trade and foreign direct investment—were hit hard during the financial crisis, but neither has suffered a similar decline since then. Trade experienced a large drop-off in 2015, but that was almost entirely a price effect, driven by plunging commodity prices and the rising value of the US dollar. Updated data suggests that in 2016 foreign direct investment dipped, in part because of the US crackdown on tax inversions. Complete data for 2016 is not yet available, but factoring in people and information flows will probably reinforce the conclusion that globalization has stayed flat or even increased.

What has nose-dived, however, is the tone of public discourse in the United States and other advanced economies. An analysis of media mentions for the term "globalization" across several major newspapers—the *Wall Street Journal,* the *New York Times,* and the *Washington Post* in the US and the *Times of London,* the *Guardian,* and the *Financial Times* in the UK—reveals a marked souring of sentiment, with scores plummeting in 2016.

The contrast between the mixed-to-positive data on actual international flows and the sharply negative swing in the discourse about globalization may be rooted, ironically, in the tendency of even experienced executives to greatly overestimate the intensity of international business flows relative to domestic activity. In other words, they believe the world is a lot more globalized than it actually is.

Exaggerated perceptions about the *depth* of globalization—that is, how much activity is international versus domestic—come at a cost. In surveys I've conducted, respondents who overestimated the intensity of globalization were more likely to believe erroneous statements about international business strategy and public policy. When businesspeople think the world is more globalized than it really is, they tend to underestimate the need to understand and respond to differences across countries when operating abroad. In the public policy sphere, leaders tend to underestimate the potential gains from additional globalization and to overestimate its harmful consequences for society.

Surveys suggest that people also underestimate the *breadth* of globalization—that is, the extent to which international activity is distributed globally rather than narrowly focused. In a 2007 survey of *Harvard Business Review* readers, 62% of respondents agreed with the quote from Thomas Friedman's best-selling book *The World Is Flat* that companies now operate on "a global, Web-enabled playing field that allows for … collaboration on research and work in real time, without regard to geography, distance or, in the near future, even language." However, data shows that actual international activity continues to be dampened strongly by all those factors.

To counteract such "globaloney," I offer two laws that govern, respectively, the depth and breadth of globalization:

- The law of semi-globalization: International business activity, while significant, is much less intense than domestic activity.
- The law of distance: International interactions are dampened by distance along cultural, administrative, geographic, and, often, economic dimensions.

These principles, set out in my book *The Laws of Globalization,* can be very helpful for strategy making—if they can be counted on to apply in the future. Given surging protectionist sentiments and possibly even a trade war, will they continue to hold? The best way of stress-testing them—at a time when the precise policies of the Trump administration and other governments are still unclear—is to look at the last time a major trade war broke out, in the 1930s, which led to the largest reversal of globalization in history. Two major lessons, corresponding to the two laws of globalization, stand out.

The first lesson is that although trade dropped precipitously in the 1930s, it did not dry up entirely. The collapse that began in 1929 was staggering, and by early 1933, trade flows had plummeted by two-thirds. That said, the drop-off in value reflected a fall more in prices than in quantities, which declined by less than 30%. Even in the wake of the collapse, trade volumes continued to be far too large for business strategists to ignore.

The second lesson is that distance of various sorts continued to dampen international business activity. For example, from 1928 to

1935, the relationship between trade flows and geographic distance barely budged. The beneficial effects of a common language and colonial ties remained powerful: Country pairs with such ties continued to trade about five times as much with each other as pairs without such ties, all else being equal. The net result was that the trading partners with whom countries (or groups of countries) did most of their business before the crash remained largely unchanged afterward.

Getting back to the future: If global trade didn't screech to a halt in the 1930s, it's reasonably safe to say that it won't in the 2020s, either. In fact, analyses of what a trade war under Trump might look like suggest much smaller declines in trade than occurred in the 1930s. Moody's Analytics estimates that if the United States were to impose proposed tariffs on China and Mexico and those two countries retaliated in kind, that and other factors would shrink US exports by $85 billion in 2019. That's only about 4% of total US exports in 2015. Of course, a wider trade war would have a more significant effect, but it is very unlikely that the consequences would be as dire as in the 1930s.

Similarly, if the breadth of trade didn't change much despite the drastic declines in depth during the Great Depression, it probably wouldn't change much in the event of a trade war today. It is worth adding that with many more independent countries now, as well as more vertically fragmented supply chains, the estimated effects of geographic distance on merchandise trade are actually larger than they were in the 1930s.

Critics of Global Capitalism and Free Trade Are Missing the Bigger Picture

Michael Matheson Miller

Michael Matheson Miller is a research fellow at the Acton Institute. His written work has appeared in numerous publications, including the Washington Times, *the* Detroit News, *and* RealClearPolitics.

One of the most enduring critiques of capitalism is that it is morally and culturally corrosive. Even if we grant that capitalism is more efficient than planned economies, the question remains: are the economic gains worth the cultural cost? Now if the critique came only from a handful of Marxist academics who long for the good ol' days of the Soviet Union, it might tempting to ignore it. But since the cultural critique comes from political observers at almost every point on the political spectrum, and since the bureaucratic-capitalist economies of the world really are cultures in crisis, the criticism is worth attending to seriously.

If we are going to analyze the cultural effects of market economies then I think that one of the first things we need to do is distinguish between those things Peter Berger called "intrinsic" to capitalism and those "extrinsic" to it. We need to distinguish among at least three things:

1. the cultural effects *caused* by capitalism,
2. effects *aided* and *abetted* by capitalism,
3. and those things that exist alongside capitalism and are often *conflated* with capitalism, but that are distinct from it.

I will say from the outset that I support open, competitive economies that allow for free exchange, but I would not call myself a "capitalist." Capitalism is generally a Marxist term that

"Does Capitalism Destroy Culture?" by Michael Matheson Miller, Intercollegiate Studies Institute, Inc., July 17, 2018. Reprinted by permission.

implies a mechanistic view of the economy and a false dichotomy between "capital" and "labor." Capitalism also comes in a variety of forms and can mean many things. There is corporate capitalism, oligarchic capitalism, crony capitalism, and managerial-bureaucratic capitalism, such as we have in the United States. However, cultural critics of capitalism usually don't make those distinctions and, even if they did, many would still be critical of an authentically free market.

So without trying to tease apart all of these strands at the outset and so risk never getting anywhere let me use the term "capitalism" and ask and answer the question with the broadest of brushstrokes. Does capitalism corrode culture? I think the answer is yes and no.

Creative Destruction

Perhaps the first cultural critique of capitalism is that it destroys traditional culture and ways of living. Much of the answer depends upon what we mean by traditional culture, but generally the answer is clearly yes. Competitive global market economies undoubtedly transform traditional cultures, and this is not limited to far off places in Africa, Latin America, or the Polynesian Islands. In the history of Western Europe and the United States, market economies played a vital role in transforming traditions and radically altering social interaction.

One of the main ways the market does this is through *innovation*. As new technologies, industries, and goods and services emerge, they make older ones obsolete; old industries are shut down and new ones emerge. New forms of management and technology and division of labor transform traditional work and social relations, and new technologies alter traditional roles of women and men in the house. These sweeping changes can also destroy traditional work and social relationships that play an essential cultural and economic role in the lives of a community or nation. At the same time it is important not to understate the real positive social benefits that come from economic growth and the reduction of extreme poverty. This is what Joseph Schumpeter called "creative destruction," and it would be naïve to deny that creative destruction doesn't come with serious trade-offs.

Some traditional and artisanal trades are lost forever and this can be a cultural impoverishment. At the same time, because we associate global capitalism with modernization we assume it only has negative effects on traditional culture. Yet there are cases when the opening of markets has actually enhanced local cultural production. As Tyler Cowen notes in *Creative Destruction*, global trade and new imports have stimulated the local music industry in Ghana where local musicians now control about 70 percent of the Ghanaian market. Global markets have also provided producers of traditional goods and music a bigger market to sell their wares and take advantages of economies of scale.

When I was in Rwanda I interviewed Janet Nkbana, a entrepreneur who produces traditional baskets and sells them not only locally but at Macy's in the United States. As more people travel and live abroad and tastes become more eclectic, Janet has potential consumers she would never have if her market were limited to Rwanda. Her business success has also brought with it positive social benefits to her community. Though basket making is a traditionally female industry, her company's success has attracted Rwandan men to seek employment, and this has not only raised family incomes, but also reduced the incidents of alcoholism and violence against women and children. This is an example of cultural transformation afforded by global capitalism, and it is clearly a positive one.

Homogenizing Homo Sapiens

Related to the critique that capitalism destroys traditional culture is the argument that global capitalism is a leveling force that is making the whole world homogenous and Westernized. There is partial truth to this and any visit to an American suburb each with its own Home Depot, Lowe's, and Walmart bears this out. But there are other things going on too. We see the rise of specialty stores, plenty of different restaurants with cuisine from all over the world and a variety of choices that did not exist fifty years ago.

It is a mistake to conflate modernization and broad use of technology with Westernization. A young Asian eating McDonald's while listening to an iPod likely knows little if anything about the culture, traditions, and religion that shaped Western civilization and set the ground for technological developments that he enjoys. There are traditional Muslims and Buddhists who work in technology sectors, but have absorbed little or nothing of Western culture. The use of modern technology does not make one a Westerner any more than the use of Japanese technology educates one about Zen, *tataemae, senpai-kohai, obon,* or Shintoism. The world may be less flat than we imagine.

One of the most passionate critiques of capitalism is really aimed at something else: industrialization. Capitalism and industrialization are related, of course, but they are not the same thing. The rise of capitalism predates the industrial revolution by centuries. As Rodney Stark and Raymond de Roover have noted, international banking and a capitalist economy emerged in Northern Italy as early as the 8th century, and among the Dutch and English and other parts of Europe by the high Middle Ages. Even more obviously, industrialization has taken place in non-capitalist societies like the Soviet Union and communist China, and at times with a soul-crushing aridity that makes an American mall seem aesthetically pleasing by comparison. The reality is, many of the critiques of modern capitalism, especially aesthetic and cultural critiques, are more precisely critiques of industrialism than of capitalism or the free market per se.

Cultural Imperialism

Finally, while capitalism does indeed transform, and even destroy, aspects of traditional cultural life, I would argue that the most destructive global forces of cultural transformation especially in the developing world come less from market economies than from the Western, secular, organizations like the United Nations, the World

Bank, the NGO industry, and the US and European governments. These powerful institutions wield "soft" and "hard" power to foist a reductionist vision of life upon millions of the world's poor. People criticize McDonald's and Walmart for cultural imperialism, but no one is forced to eat a Big Mac. Contrast this to activities of groups like the UN, UNICEF and Planned Parenthood, who impose secular ideas of family, motherhood, sexuality, abortion, contraception, and forced sterilization on the world's poor. It is bad enough when a country like China does this to their own people, but when bureaucrats in Washington or Paris are manipulating poor families in the developing world, and tying aid packages to so called reproductive rights it is a naked act of cultural imperialism.

There now exists what the *New York Times* has called a "daughter deficit" and what *The Economist* has labeled "gendercide." Millions of baby girls are being aborted in the developing world as people are encouraged by international agencies and NGOs to have small families. For a variety of cultural reasons, when forced to choose, many of the families choose to have baby boys and abort their unborn daughters. The consequences of the loss of all these human lives is of course incalculable, but that isn't the extent of it. The birth ratio of boys to girls is now so skewed that this will have devastating social and political consequences.

This is not the result of free markets. It is a product of selfish consumerism, bad anthropology and faulty economics—an outgrowth [of] decades of educational policy and top-down social and economic planning that grows out of the zero-sum-game fallacy, which in turn fosters an anti-natalist ideology that dominates development insiders. Not surprisingly, these insiders are rarely proponents of the free market, and if they do give the market a nod it is a kind of techno-bureaucratic capitalism ruled by elites who haunt Davos each year.

Solipsistic Individualism and Consumerism

Critics also charge capitalism with promoting radical concepts of autonomy, such as the type of entrepreneurs untethered from moral absolutes portrayed in *The Social Network*. This type was evident among some bankers during the financial crisis and still is among techno-utopian entrepreneurs who believe they can re-engineer the human soul and even escape death itself through technology. While the market does enable people to indulge in a lifestyle marked by the illusion of radical autonomy, the main sources of such thinking and behavior are not market economics, but a number of harder to diagnose intellectual and spiritual crises that plague the west. These include things like *reductionist rationalism* that makes all questions of truth, beauty, and the good life a matter of personal predilection; a *nominalist* conception of human freedom where freedom is merely the exercise of the will separated from truth and reason; the radical *individualism* of Hobbes, Locke, and Rousseau; and radical skepticism (see David Hume) which makes reason a slave to the passions.

A market economy can help spread these ideas, but it is not their source. I am not arguing that a market is neutral. Markets have clear positive and negative effects, but exacerbating a problem is not the same thing as causing it and it is simplistic to attribute to capitalism alone the effects of a host of intertwined forces of social change. Perhaps the most powerful critique of capitalism is its relationship to consumerism. The consumerist ethic, with its hyper-sexuality and advertising to young children is especially troubling. In *Born to Buy*, Boston University Professor Juliet Schor details the marketing and advertising that bypasses parents and tries to market directly to children as young as three and four years old. Companies spend millions in marketing research and advertising to every age category from toddler to a new category called "tween" to the seemingly ubiquitous marketing aimed at teenagers in mega-malls. Benjamin Barber in his book *Consumed*, reports that "businesses spend over $11 billion per year advertising to children, teens, and young adults." Barber also discusses the troubling trend of individuals defining themselves by the brands they use. Brands, he argues, have replaced families, religion, and communities as a source of identity. He writes, "The boundary separating the person from what she buys starts to vanish—and she starts to become the products she buys—a Calvin Klein torrid teen, a politically conscious Benetton rebel." These are serious problems.

But the question again is whether this is the result of the free market *per se*? There is undoubtedly a relationship between the two, yet consumerism exists in socialist societies as well. There have also been capitalist societies that have not been consumerist and have encouraged high levels of savings and investment. As several commentators including William Leach in *Land of Desire* have noted, America has seen a cultural shift from *productive capitalism* with focus on saving and investment to a consumerist mentality where we consume on borrowed money. The reasons for this are a complex interaction of cultural shifts, education, increased individualism and centralization, much of it incentivized by public and monetary policy (Keynesianism) which have encouraged consumerism and borrowing. Consumerism is a toxic malady and will undermine a free society. Wilhelm Röpke, the Swiss economist who was instrumental in rebuilding German after World War II and an ardent free marketer, once asked if there was "any more certain way of desiccating the soul of man than the habit of constantly thinking about money and what it can buy? Is there a more potent poison than our economic system's all pervasive commercialism?"

A market economy with an abundance of goods can encourage consumerism, and while policies that limit vulgarity and abuse in advertising can help, consumerism is ultimately a spiritual disease that cannot be remedied by economic changes alone.

Does the Economy Control Culture?

The relationship between capitalism and culture is complex. Competitive free market economies have helped secure liberty and have lifted more people out of poverty than any alternative. With that progress has come great volatility and accelerated social change that is undeniable. However, blaming capitalism is much easier than addressing the actual, but harder-to-diagnose sources of cultural breakdown. Capitalism becomes an easy scapegoat for several reasons.

1. First, there remains a tendency toward economic determinism influenced by Marxian analysis which views the economy as the source of social organization. This is not limited to the left. Distributists for example, who are quite traditional and religious, tend to appropriate the Marxian view of the economy as the driving force of culture and thereby see structural economic change as the source of cultural renewal.

2. Second, capitalism often becomes a proxy for a critique of problems that lie deep within modern liberal society such as the effects of nominalism, rationalism, radical concepts of autonomy and the like. It is much easier to blame inanimate market forces than to attempt to dissect the effects of nominalism and Enlightenment rationalism on culture and social relations.

3. Finally, capitalism also acts as a proxy for other issues which would be politically incorrect or at least politically imprudent to address directly. Criticizing capitalism is easier and more politically acceptable than it would be to critique democracy, egalitarianism, or the welfare state. Alexis de Tocqueville, for example, worried about the negative effects of equality and individualism on culture and the human soul and that equality led to a love of comfort. Can you imagine a contemporary politician in the United States or Europe standing up today and talking about the dangers of too much equality or democracy? What would happen if a politician blamed consumerism on equality instead of corporate greed?

Capitalism has profound effects on culture and it is a mistake to think that that the market economy is neutral or that markets left to their own devices will work everything out for the best. It is also a mistake to blame capitalism as the cause of cultural destruction. Market economies come with trade-offs and cultural dysfunction and cultural renewal are complex and cannot be explained by economic analysis alone. As Christopher Dawson reminds us, it is not economics, but *cultus,* religion, that is the driving force of culture. It is also a mistake to think that secularism is neutral. Modern secular progressivism has become the *cultus* of Western life and this plays a much more potent role in shaping culture than economics.

Capitalism is not perfect. Like democracy, it needs vibrant mediating institutions, rich civil society and a strong religious culture to control its negative effects. But we wouldn't trade democracy for dictatorship. Nor should we trade the market for some bureaucratic utopia. For all their fallen, human faults, free and competitive economies have enabled millions of people to lead lives of human dignity and pursue human flourishing, and funded the creation of beautiful architecture, music, and cultural products of all sorts. If we are going to take cultural decay seriously then simply blaming capitalism will not get us very far.

There are much bigger fish to fry.

Protectionism Harms Consumers and Workers

The World Bank Group

The World Bank Group is an international financial institution that provides loans to developing countries. It was founded in 1944.

More than twenty-five years of progressive liberalization of trade, from 1947 to 1974, saw unprecedented growth in world prosperity. Then the economic climate changed for the worse. Currency crises, oil crises, debt crises, world recession, and high unemployment produced an atmosphere in which demands for protection increased dramatically. The success of Japanese exports, and then of exports from the newly industrializing countries (NICs), produced pressure for changes in the older industrial nations. Such changes are painful when unemployment is high. Attempts to avoid the pain are the main cause of today's protectionism in the industrial countries. Trade in textiles was the first victim, followed closely by trade in footwear, leather goods, steel, shipbuilding, cars, and consumer electronics.

Instead of tariffs, which are now very low, the main instrument of recent protection has been the nontariff barrier (NTB). It contravenes widely accepted principles of nondiscrimination and transparency in measures to restrict trade principles which remain sound. NTBs usually discriminate against the lowest-cost sources of imports, so they raise prices to consumers and keep inefficient industries in business. The costs to the country imposing the NTB, and to the world as a whole, are higher than under an equivalent tariff. Moreover, NTBs are unfair, because they do not treat exporters equally. Often it is the exporters with the least bargaining power whose exports are most reduced.

"The Threat of Protectionism," The World Bank Group, 1987. https://openknowledge .worldbank.org/bitstream/handle/10986/5970/9780195205633_ch08.pdf. Licensed under CC BY 3.0 IGO.

Although demands for protection have proliferated and the quantity of trade covered by nontariff barriers has increased, the effects on trade are not easy to quantify. Many trade barriers have proved porous: businessmen in the Republic of Korea and Hong Kong, for example, have to some extent overcome the restrictive effects of NTBs, and their exports of manufactures have continued to grow. But the latest Multifibre Arrangement (MFA) has broader coverage and tighter restrictions than its predecessors. New exporters will find its barriers harder to penetrate. If protection in the industrial nations increases still further, it will be hard for the developing countries to expand their exports.

Although the developing countries have been able to avoid some of the effects of industrial countries' protection, the industrial countries themselves have not. Clearly the main costs of protection fall on the importing country. NTBs cause higher prices for consumers, lost tariff revenue for governments, inefficient resource allocation, and diminished competition.

The pattern of trade cannot remain static. Since the early 1960s developing countries have been increasing their exports not only to industrial countries but also to other developing countries. Today their exports account for nearly one-third of world exports to developing countries. They have also expanded trade with the centrally planned economies (CPEs), although these exports have stagnated in the past few years. But it remains unlikely that exports to these other countries will expand enough to lessen the importance of industrial country markets or the significance of the threat of industrial country protectionism.

The international trading system since World War II has, at least in principle, been guided by the rules and procedures agreed to by the signatories to the General Agreement on Tariffs and Trade (GATT). The GATT is simply an agreement signed by member nations which are admitted on the basis of their willingness to accept the GATT disciplines; it provides rules governing trade between the signatories, a forum for negotiations, and mechanisms for resolving disputes. As a legal document it is detailed, complex, and in various areas open to differing interpretations. But the main objectives are the reduction of trade barriers and the prevention of discrimination in trade. The means by which these objectives have been pursued in the GATT include: first, successive rounds of trade negotiations about tariffs, other barriers to trade, and specific disputes; second, the GATT rule of most favored nation (MFN) treatment, which says that the lowest tariff (or other trade barrier) applied by a signatory to the GATT on a product must be applied to all signatories; third, the principle of reciprocity, whereby trade barriers are lowered in return for changes of rough equivalence by trading partners.

[…]

The Increase in Protectionist Measures

From the end of World War II until 1974 the United States was a force for trade liberalization. It adopted special measures of protection for manufacturing in only two instances, apart from the cotton textiles arrangement. These, for canned tuna in 1951 and carbon steel in 1969, involved only a tiny fraction of total US imports. Since 1974, however, there have been many more such measures. Most of them are concentrated on textiles and clothing, steel, cars, motorcycles, nonrubber footwear, color televisions, and citizens band radios. This is generally true of all industrial countries' restrictions on imports of manufactures. Agricultural and fuel imports are also subject to NTBs in most industrial countries. Barriers against goods such as these mainly affect the exports of other industrial countries. Only Brazil and Korea are significant exporters of steel and automobiles; several other developing countries are affected by NTBs on consumer electronics.

The barriers which most affect many developing countries are the NTBs against textiles and clothing. The manufacture of these products seemed suitable for many developing countries because, at least until quite recently, the technologies were simple and relatively labor-intensive. Textiles and clothing represent approximately

25 percent of developing countries' manufactured exports. Each successive version of the MFA has been more restrictive and has covered more products and exporters.

A detailed analysis of the extent of NTBs has been carried out by staff of the World Bank using the UNCTAD/World Bank data base on trade measures. It showed that about 17 percent of industrial countries' imports in 1986 were subject to "hardcore" NTBs.

In addition to the formal restrictions shown in the table, many countries make use of other devices to protect domestic interests. France, for example, used an administrative measure to restrict the imports of videocassette recorders.

The study also showed that NTBs bear more heavily on the major exports of developing countries than on similar exports from industrial market economies, mainly because of the much greater importance of textiles and clothing in the exports of developing countries. Nontariff measures increased significantly between 1981 and 1986, particularly in Canada, the EC, and the United States. Some $230 billion of 1981 imports would have been covered by one or more of the selected NTBs as they applied in 1983. Post-Tokyo Round tariffs are now so low on most goods that they represent relatively minor barriers to trade. Even where they remain high, as on textiles and garments, the binding constraint on trade is normally bilateral quotas and voluntary export restraints (VERs) under the MFA.

Explanations for the Growth of Protectionism

Why has the movement toward a more liberal trading environment stalled? Is the new protectionism a temporary response to the current crisis or the beginning of a new trend brought about by a lack of faith in an open trading system? If the former, the tide of protectionism may ebb with economic recovery. But if major countries no longer feel that their interests are served by the GATT rules, then an open trading system is indeed in peril.

The Demand for Protection

Protection is demanded by groups who see their interests damaged by imports and is supplied by governments that see their interests served by giving way to these demands. Economic arguments play a role, but probably a minor one. The demand for protection has usually involved an alliance of owners and workers (although the internationalization of production through multinational corporations and international subcontracting may be undermining such alliances to some extent). Three factors seem likely to have stimulated such domestic interest groups to demand protection in recent years:

- Structural changes in trade. Japan's dependence on imports of energy and raw materials forced it to become an even more aggressive exporter of manufactures in response to the oil crises and a slowdown in growth. Since 1978 it has consistently had a trade surplus. The rise in Japan's share of imports of manufactures from other members of the Organisation for Economic Co-Operation and Development (OECD) coincided with an increase in the NICs' share from 1980 onward; the pressure on some OECD countries' import-competing industries was great.

- The growth in intra-OECD trade in the 1960s and 1970s was largely in intraindustry trade. This meant there was less need to adjust. No industries needed to shrink to accommodate imports because they were able to expand exports. But the exports of the NICs tend to be labor-intensive and concentrated on a few products: textiles, clothing, foot-wear, leather, and sporting goods. They import machinery and sophisticated manufactures. Even though the overall balance of trade with the NICs is positive, certain OECD industries are under intense pressure from the NICs' highly competitive exports; the labor displaced may not be easily reabsorbed by exports. The OECD countries' imports from developing countries have a higher direct labor content than their imports from other OECD countries. The ratios imply that a billion dollar increase in OECD exports would not create enough jobs to absorb the labor displaced by a billion dollar increase in developing country imports. (But, if such a matched expansion of trade did occur, real incomes would rise, demand would increase, and jobs would be created in other OECD industries.)

- The new markets created in the NICs for OECD exports are intensely competitive. There are no brand loyalties, and costs of entry are low. This has led OECD exporters to demand help from their governments. The help could be subsidized loans, measures to tie trade to aid projects, or other forms of concealed assistance to exporters.

- Reduced flexibility. Labor markets in Britain and some other European nations have changed in ways which have made labor less mobile between occupations and regions. Because the impact of NIC exports is mainly on industries which tend to be labor-intensive and concentrated in regions of high unemployment (textiles, clothing, and leather goods), labor market rigidities cause demands for protection.

- Effects of recession and instability in the international economy. Slowly growing economies find adjustment more difficult and painful than economies which are growing rapidly. They lack the expansion of new activities to absorb the labor displaced from their "twilight" industries. High average levels of unemployment increase the net costs of losing a job and make governments more sensitive to unemployment caused by imports. All this reinforces demands for protection.

- Misaligned exchange rates. In the 1980s, in both Britain and the United States, appreciating exchange rates meant that import-competing and export industries suffered a severe loss of competitiveness. Producers and politicians responded with louder demands for protection. Unfortunately, the recent depreciation of the dollar has failed to stifle these demands.

Recent Arguments Used to Justify Special Protection

Those who demand protection offer several economic arguments in support. For the most part, these are merely variants on the traditional case for protection. But as advanced by the industrial countries, some take on a different slant.

Maintaining Employment

If a rise in imports causes the sales of an industry to contract, protecting that industry can, at least in the short run, help to maintain jobs. But this neglects the effect of the resulting price increase on demand, focuses too narrowly on the directly affected industry, and pays no attention to the unintended effects of the protection on other industries, if the protected industry is a source of inputs to other industries, then tariffs or controls on imports will raise costs and reduce employment in the industries which use the protected materials. Their job losses may exceed those temporarily saved in the protected industries.

Moreover, if the exchange rate is flexible, an increase in protection which reduces expenditure on imports will, if nothing else changes, cause the exchange rate to appreciate. This will reduce profits in both exporting and import-substituting industries, which would cause employment to fall in all tradable goods industries apart from those given the increased protection. If, in addition, trading partners react to the protection by increasing their own trade barriers, the protection to save jobs would be not only self-defeating but potentially disastrous.

What at first seems self-evident that protecting an industry against a surge in imports will save jobs turns out to be a risky proposition.

Slowing the Pace of Adjustment

A modification of the employment argument carries more weight. The idea is to use temporary controls to allow a slower pace of adjustment on the grounds that resources may not be very mobile and that time may be required to retrain labor and allow new investment to take place. The need to slow down adjustment is acknowledged by the inclusion of safeguard provisions in most trade treaties such as the GATT and the Treaty of Rome. The argument is valid, but it can be used to justify protection which is far from temporary and in situations where no effort is made to shift resources from the area in which comparative advantage has been lost.

Preserving the Incomes of Certain Groups

This is one of the main arguments used for the protection of agriculture in industrial nations. As *World Development Report 1986* showed, the main effect of such a policy is to push up the price of land, which benefits only landowners. Direct income support would be more successful in preserving wages in farming at a much lower real cost to the community. In other industries, where there is no factor of production in fixed supply, such as land, there is no reason in principle why incomes could not be supported by protecting the industry, but direct income transfers would still be far less costly.

Preserving Key Industries

Protection for agriculture, steel, and automobiles is frequently buttressed with the idea that these industries have strategic importance. One industrial country has argued that its clothing industry is essential for defense because it produces uniforms for the army. This shows the lengths to which the argument has been pushed. For many products stockpiling is a cheaper way to preserve supplies for emergencies than protecting the industry. If an industry really is essential, the question is how best to preserve it. The orthodox economic answer is through subsidies, not tariffs or import controls. Subsidies do not raise prices, hurt consumers, or raise costs to users. But the precedents are ominous. Subsidies often get out of hand and play havoc with budgets.

Some industries are claimed to be essential for economic reasons. It is not clear why a country should need its own aircraft industry or computer industry if it can buy more cheaply from foreign suppliers. But one extension of this argument may be defensible. If allowing these domestic producers to collapse meant the creation of a worldwide monopoly, which could then raise prices to very high levels, a case for subsidies to preserve some competition could be made. But this would be a special and somewhat speculative case.

Supporting New (High Technology) Industries

One variant of the infant industry argument cites the need to assist new industries through the learning period (when the local industry cannot compete with already established foreign firms). Another variant relies on external benefits such as technical spin-offs as a justification for protection. The learning period argument is subject to the standard criticism that it implies a failure in the capital market. Otherwise, if an industry cannot attract adequate capital to see it through this learning period, investors evidently cannot be convinced that it offers a competitive rate of return. It is implausible that the capital markets of the industrial nations suffer from such weaknesses. True, because of misinformation or inadequate information investors can make mistakes, but why should that be any less true of governments, whose economic vision may be clouded by political requirements?

External economies are another matter. In this case governments, provided they are well informed and pursue the public well-being in a disinterested way, are necessarily superior to markets because market prices cannot capture genuine externalities.

Using Protection as a Lever to Open Markets

Recently, some industrial countries have used the threat of protection as a lever to open other countries' markets. At first glance this seems an almost benign strategy, opening markets to trade rather than closing markets by protection. But it is yet another step down the road to managed trade. Each individual bilateral trade deal may seem insignificant, but it invites further political action of the same kind and undermines the system of rules governing trade in the GATT. Such arrangements may in any case backfire, as happened with the US-Japan accord on trade in semiconductors. US firms suffered rather than gained from the protection. The failures of the accord seem to have sown the seeds of further conflict.

Combatting Unfair Trade

There have been increasing demands in industrial countries for "fair trade" rather than free trade. Normally, unfair trade practices mean such things as nontariff barriers, covert means to restrict imports, government subsidies (direct or indirect) to exports, and dumping (selling to export markets below the price in domestic markets). Demands that trade should take place on "a level playing field" sometimes go beyond the question of unfair practices and attack the very basis of trade differences in comparative advantage. For example, in pleading for stiffer protection of the garment industry, a labor union representative in the United States put forward a common view: "Apparel produced in countries with abysmally low living standards and virtually no workers' rights threatens living standards in this country and destroys badly needed employment opportunities for our low-skilled workers" (US Congress, House Committee on Energy and Commerce 1985, p. 81). But protecting US garment production will, at best, preserve jobs and incomes for garment workers only at the cost of jobs and incomes elsewhere in the economy and will make it more difficult for workers in developing countries to raise their "abysmally low" living standards.

The Supply of Protection

A combination of domestic and international factors seems likely to influence the readiness of governments to be persuaded by such arguments and to accede to demands for protection. Policymakers are influenced by the relative power and persuasiveness of different interest groups in the economy. On the side of protection are the injured import-competing industries. On the other side are users of imported products: consumers; retailers; industries, including multinational corporations which use the products as inputs; and exporting firms. In the past, opponents of protection have found it hard to organize effective lobbying against it. The costs of protection seem too small and too diffuse to arouse public opinion, whereas the benefits, such as jobs saved directly in the threatened industries, have appealed to public sentiment.

Domestic Factors

The willingness of policymakers to respond to demands for trade barriers depends partly on the alternatives at their disposal. For most of the postwar era, governments have responded to rising unemployment with expansionary policies to create new jobs or with regional policies to switch investment to new activities in the area where unemployment had risen. In France, Italy, and the United Kingdom, regional policies were used vigorously in the 1950s and 1960s. By creating new jobs in the electrical goods and other light manufacturing industries, they probably helped to cope with some of the labor displaced by competition from textile imports and the loss of shipbuilding orders to Japan and Sweden. (Whether regional policies brought net gains to these economies is a subject of considerable controversy.) The much tighter fiscal restraints imposed upon governments by the need to control inflation and reduce tax burdens in the 1970s and 1980s have reduced their ability to use fiscal policies to expand demand and to increase subsidies. In the United States, the policies to assist adjustment which were introduced in the trade act that preceded the Kennedy Round have provoked considerable disillusionment, although the United States still favors the principle. Other countries, such as the Netherlands, have experimented with special assistance for import-displaced workers; they too have been less than satisfied. As their policy options have narrowed, governments have been more willing to concede to demands for protection.

International Factors

Risk of retaliation also influences governments. The United States and the EC are important customers for each other's exports. Both sides have used retaliation, or the threat of it, to attack barriers against their exports. Most of the developing countries import relatively few manufactures for consumption. The goods they import from OECD nations tend to be necessary inputs into their own production. This makes it difficult for them to produce a credible retaliatory threat. The inability to retaliate may be one reason the developing countries now face the tough bilateral constraints of the MFA in textiles and other NTBs in agriculture, footwear, and leather goods. The combination of increasing demands for protection and governments' diminishing will to resist accounts for the rise of the new protectionism in the 1970s and 1980s. The current multilateral negotiations in the Uruguay Round are an opportunity to check this trend, but that can happen only if governments make a determined effort.

[…]

Net Costs to Developing Countries of Industrial Countries' Protection

The fact that the industrial countries' NTBs have been porous does not mean that they have done no economic harm. Clearly, they have forced developing country exporters to adopt stratagems which they would not choose in either a free trade environment or one in which trade restrictions are nondiscriminatory. Protection frustrates comparative advantage. It shores up dying industries and slows the development of new ones. It diverts energies to rent seeking.

Estimating the Effects

Few studies exist of the costs of protection to developing countries. And they measure only one aspect of the costs: the increase in export earnings which would arise from reduced tariffs and NTBs. Studies by the World Bank, the IMF, and the Commonwealth Secretariat show that the result would be substantial export gains worth several billion dollars a year.

There have been more detailed studies for individual countries such as Korea. Restrictions on Korean exports of carbon steel cut sales to the United States by $207 million, or 24 percent; but Korea had offsetting gains in the form of higher prices and increased sales to other markets, and the end result may have been a small net gain.

Hong Kong faces quantitative restrictions on many of its exports. It seems unique in permitting firms to trade their quota rights. The prices offered for these are a good indicator of the rent which firms expect to earn from the right to export their permitted share. This, together with information on import and export unit values, enables estimates to be made of both the quota rents and the import tariff equivalents of the restrictions. They show gains of $724.6 million over the two years 1982–1983 equivalent to 1.4 percent of Hong Kong's GDP.

Such large gains are unusual. Hong Kong is a small economy with a high ratio of manufactured exports to income. For other economies the rents would be much less significant. And the quota rents are not pure gain. They arise from restrictions on exports, so although profits may rise, jobs and wages in these labor-intensive industries are likely to contract.

Evidence on the Costs of Protection

The costs of protection are complex. Most analysts have contented themselves with measuring only the simplest ones, and these are difficult enough. Estimates generally ignore the effects of competition on managerial efficiency, or of trade on the acquisition of new techniques, on economies of scale, on saving, and on investment. As a result, most estimates are probably too low. Most, however, also omit the adjustment costs incurred when protection is removed. But these are normally short-run, once-and-for-all costs whereas the gains from trade go on indefinitely.

Costs to Consumers

For textiles and clothing, all of the estimates for costs to consumers for the United States amounted to many billions of dollars. The same is true for standard grades of steel. For cars the estimates are just over $1 billion for the United States and $265 million for the

United Kingdom. For the EC the cost of protecting video-cassette recorders is estimated at nearly half a billion dollars.

Welfare Costs

This concept recognizes that what matters is the extra cost to the economy as a whole of producing more of the goods domestically rather than importing them. It is a net cost, because the extra price paid by consumers goes partly to local producers whose production expands to replace imports and partly to the government in revenue from the tariff. (Where protection is by quotas, importers will usually gain at the expense of consumers. Where it is by VERs, foreign suppliers will normally capture the benefit of the increased price.) Normally, the welfare cost will be considerably less than the consumer cost particularly for tariffs or quotas. Even so, the estimates for textiles and clothing range from $1.4 billion to $6.6 billion in the EC and the United States, and for steel in the United States the estimate is approximately $2 billion.

The Cost of Preserving a Job

The striking fact about protection to preserve jobs is that each job often ends up costing consumers more than the worker's salary. For example, each job preserved in the car industry in Britain is estimated to have cost consumers between $19,000 and $48,000 a year. In the United States the cost was between $40,000 and $108,500 a year. Looked at another way, in the United Kingdom the cost to consumers of preserving one worker in car production was equivalent to four workers earning the average industrial wage in other industries. In the US car industry, the equivalent cost would be the wages of six ordinary industrial workers. VERs in the US steel industry cost consumers $114,000 per protected job each year. For every dollar paid to steelworkers who would have lost their jobs, consumers lost $35 and the US economy as a whole lost $25.

Are Jobs Really Saved?

It is of course questionable whether protection can do any more than temporarily preserve some jobs in the protected industry at the expense of jobs in other industries in the economy. The extra cash spent on steel and VCRs implies less cash to spend on other goods and services and therefore fewer jobs in production of these other goods and services. Even in the protected sector the effects of protection on saving jobs are usually small.

British and American VERs on Japanese car exports stimulated imports of similar cars from the rest of Europe. Much of the effect of the MFA was to divert trade from some developing country suppliers to others and to other OECD suppliers. The textile industry has invested heavily in capital-intensive production methods, because of controls on imports which yielded economic rents to domestic producers and (in many countries) because of subsidies for new capital equipment. The industry's new technology has displaced workers at a much higher rate than imports. In the United States, the new jobs in textiles have been located in the South rather than in New England and are for a type of labor different from before. Geographic and skill barriers have meant that protecting textiles did little to save jobs or reduce costs of adjustment. Even when protection has a positive effect on output in the domestic industry, it tends to be small in relation to macroeconomic change. For example, the 1982 United States-Japan VER on cars is estimated to have increased demand for domestic production by 100,000 units, less than 1 percent of industry sales. By contrast, stagnation and high interest rates in the US economy reduced demand by about 4 million units in 1982 compared with 1978.

Protection has not been particularly successful in maintaining jobs or reducing adjustment costs even in the protected industry. For the economy as a whole, because of the intersectoral and macroeconomic effects, it probably lowered employment. Few jobs have been saved, and the costs have been inordinate.

Conclusion

Protectionism has been growing since the mid-1970s. Measures such as VERs and orderly marketing arrangements have been porous. The NICs and some other developing countries have been ingenious in finding ways to penetrate these measures or to turn them to their advantage. Nevertheless, the measures have had adverse effects. The increased coverage and tighter administration of the MFA and increased vigilance in administering NTBs may mean worse to come. As it is, protection has diverted trade from developing country exporters to OECD suppliers. The response of the developing countries has not been costless.

The industrial countries bear the main costs of their own protection. Estimates of the costs seem small in relation to GNP, but they are probably underestimates. Moreover, the appropriate test is not to compare the costs with GNP. As with any economic policy, protection should be evaluated on the balance of costs and benefits. On that basis protection should win few friends.

Traditionally, pressure for protection eases when a new round of trade negotiations is in the offing. This reinforces the need to make a success of the new multilateral trade negotiations. The best way to overcome protectionism is to renew the momentum of progress toward multilateral liberalization of trade.

Organizations to Contact

The editors have compiled the following list of organizations concerned with the issues debated in this book. The descriptions are derived from materials provided by the organizations. All have publications or information available for interested readers. This list was compiled on the date of publication of the present volume; the information provided here may change. Be aware that many organizations take several weeks or longer to respond to inquiries, so allow as much time as possible.

American Institute for Economic Research (AIER)
PO Box 1000
Great Barrington, MA 01230-1000
phone: (888) 528-1216
email: info@aier.org
website: www.aier.org

Founded in 1933, the American Institute for Economic Research (AIER) is dedicated to educating Americans on its ideals, including free trade, property rights, and limited government. AIER publishes research, hosts colloquiums, and sponsors scholarship. It is home to the Bastiat Society and the Sound Money Project.

Economic Policy Institute (EPI)
1225 Eye St. NW, Ste. 600
Washington, DC 20005
phone: (202) 775-8810
email: epi@epi.org
website: www.epi.org

The Economic Policy Institute (EPI) is a nonpartisan organization focused on spotlighting the interests of low- and middle-income workers in policy discussions that typically focus on the interests of the investment class. EPI also develops policy proposals aimed at increasing working class security and productivity.

European Centre for International Political Economy (ECIPE)
Avenue des Arts 40
1040 Brussels
Belgium
phone: +32 (0)2 289 1350
email: info@ecipe.org
website: www.ecipe.org

The European Centre for International Political Economy (ECIPE) is an independent, nonprofit think tank dedicated to the study of European economic issues. ECIPE advocates for free trade and the progressive reduction of economic barriers as a path toward greater peace, prosperity, and security across the globe.

Peterson Institute for International Economics (PIIE)
1750 Massachusetts Ave, NW
Washington, DC 20036
phone: (202) 328-9000
email: comments@piie.com
website: www.piie.com

The Peterson Institute for International Economics (PIIE) is a private, nonpartisan think tank dedicated to the study of economics, trade policy, and globalization. PIIE conducts research on emerging issues, develops policy ideas, and works to educate government officials, business leaders, and the public on international economic issues.

The World Bank
1818 H St. NW
Washington, DC 20433
phone: (202) 473-1000
website: www.worldbank.org

The World Bank provides low-interest loans and grants to developing countries to support investments in infrastructure, education, health care, and government administration. It also provides policy advice and helps connect developing countries to global sources of economic expertise and research.

World Economic Forum
350 Madison Ave., 11th Fl.
New York, NY 10017
phone: (212) 703-2300
email: forumusa@weforum.org
website: www.weforum.org

The World Economic Forum is a nonprofit organization based in Geneva. It is focused on facilitating public-private cooperation and policy agreement in the interest of promoting a healthy, stable global economic environment.

World Trade Organization (WTO)
Centre William Rappard
Rue de Lausanne, 154
Case postale
1211 Genève 2
Switzerland
phone: +41 (0)22 739 51 11
email: enquiries@wto.org
website: www.wto.org

The Geneva-based World Trade Organization (WTO) is an international organization that facilitates trade policy agreements and helps to resolve disputes between nations. Its goal is to promote a smooth, predictable, and competitive global trade environment.

Bibliography

Books

C. Fred Bergsten and Joseph Gagnon. *Currency Conflict and Trade Policy: A New Strategy for the United States.* Washington, DC: Peterson Institute for International Economics, 2017.

William J. Bernstein. *A Splendid Exchange: How Trade Shaped the World.* New York, NY: Grove Press, 2008.

Aluisio de Lima-Campos and Juan Antonio Gaviria. *Introduction to Trade Policy.* New York, NY: Routledge, 2018.

Sean D. Ehrlich. *The Politics of Fair Trade: Moving Beyond Free Trade and Protection.* New York, NY: Oxford University Press, 2018.

Elhanan Helpman. *Understanding Global Trade.* Cambridge, MA: Fellows of Harvard College, 2011.

Douglas A. Irwin. *Clashing Over Commerce: A History of US Trade Policy.* Chicago, IL: The University of Chicago Press, 2017.

Douglas A. Irwin. *Free Trade Under Fire.* Princeton, NJ: Princeton University Press, 2015.

C. Donald Johnson. *The Wealth of a Nation: A History of Trade Politics in America.* New York, NY: Oxford University Press, 2018.

Tamara Kay and R.L. Evans. *Trade Battles: Activism and the Politicization of International Trade Policy.* New York, NY: Oxford University Press, 2018.

David A. Lake. *Power, Protection, and Free Trade: International Sources of US Commercial Strategy, 1887-1939.* Ithaca, NY: Cornell University Press, 2018.

Noritsugu Nakanishi. *The Essence of International Trade Theory.* Hackensack, NJ: World Scientific Publishing Co, 2018.

Richard Pomfret. *International Trade: Theory, Evidence, and Policy.* Hackensack, NJ: World Scientific Publishing Co, 2015.

Dani Rodrik. *The Globalization Paradox: Democracy and the Future of the World Economy.* New York, NY: W. W. Norton & Company, 2011.

W. Charles Sawyer. *US International Trade Policy: An Introduction.* Santa Barbara, CA: Praeger, ABC-CLIO, 2017.

Gabriel Siles-Brugge. *Constructing European Union Trade Policy: A Global Idea of Europe.* New York, NY: Palgrave MacMillan, 2014.

Joseph E. Stiglitz. *Globalization and Its Discontents Revisited: Anti-Globalization in the Era of Trump.* New York, NY: W. W. Norton & Company, 2018.

Joseph E. Stiglitz and Mary Kaldor. *The Quest for Security: Protection Without Protectionism and the Challenge of Global Governance.* New York, NY: Columbia University Press, 2013.

Murat A. Yulek. *How Nations Succeed: Manufacturing, Trade, Industrial Policy, and Economic Development.* New York, NY: Palgrave MacMillan, 2018.

Periodicals and Internet Sources

Stuart Anderson, "Tariffs Are Costing Jobs: A Look At How Many," *Forbes*, September 24, 2018. https://www.forbes.com/sites/stuartanderson/2018/09/24/tariffs-are-costing-jobs-a-look-at-how-many/#ebeb0387b26e.

Matthew Bey, "How to Understand Trump's Trade Policy: It's About Restricting Imports," *Market Watch*, June 25, 2018. https://www.marketwatch.com/story/how-to -understand-trumps-trade-policy-its-about-restricting -imports-2018-07-25.

Jeff Desjardins, "A Brief History of US Trade Wars," *Business Insider*, July 18, 2018. https://www.businessinsider.com/a -brief-history-of-us-trade-wars-2018-7.

I. M. Destler, "America's Uneasy History with Free Trade," *Harvard Business Review*, April 28, 2016. https://hbr.org /2016/04/americas-uneasy-history-with-free-trade.

Jeff Ferry, "Contrary to Popular Belief, Trump's Tariffs Are Working," *Hill*, December 17, 2018. https://thehill.com /opinion/finance/421693-contrary-to-popular-belief -trumps-tariffs-are-working.

Jeffrey Frankel, "Trump's Trade Wars and Brexit are Making Us All Poorer," *Guardian*, November 27, 2018. https://www .theguardian.com/business/2018/nov/27/trump-trade-war -monetary-policy-central-banks.

Yuwa Hedrick-Wong, "The US-China Trade War and Global Economic Dominance," *Forbes*, September 11, 2018. https:// www.forbes.com/sites/yuwahedrickwong/2018/09/11 /the-u-s-china-trade-war-and-global-economic -dominance/#759cbba2256a.

Douglas A. Irwin, "Historical Aspects of US Trade Policy," National Bureau of Economic Research, 2006. https:// www.nber.org/reporter/summer06/irwin.html.

Lesley Kennedy, "7 Contentious Trade Wars in US History," *History.com*, September 21, 2018. https://www.history.com /news/7-trade-wars-boston-tea-party-smoot-hawley.

Peter Landers, "Japan, Germany Pledge to 'Set Boundaries' Against Trump's Trade Policies," *Market Watch*, July 25, 2018. https://www.marketwatch.com/story/japan -germany-pledge-to-set-boundaries-against-trumps-trade -policies-2018-07-25.

Heather Long, "Winners and Losers from Trump's Tariffs," *Washington Post*, March 6, 2018. https://www .washingtonpost.com/news/wonk/wp/2018/03/06/winners -and-losers-from-trumps-tariffs/?utm_term=.71b31becb529.

Annie Lowrey, "How Much Damage Will Trump's Trade War Do?" *Atlantic*, July 16, 2018. https://www.theatlantic.com /ideas/archive/2018/07/the-costs-of-trumps-trade-war /565208/.

Mary Papenfuss, "US Trade Deficit With China Hits All-Time High Despite Tariffs," *Huffington Post*, November 3, 2018. https://www.huffingtonpost.com/entry/us-trade-deficit-with -china-hits-all-time-high_us_5bdd153fe4b04367a87cb71c.

Kai Ryssal, "How US Trade Policy Has Changed Over 30 Years," *MarketPlace*, June 8, 2018. https://www.marketplace .org/2018/06/08/economy/how-us-trade-policy-has- changed-over-30-years.

Ana Swanson and Keith Bradsher, "Trump Doubles Down on Potential Trade War With China," *New York Times*, April 5, 2018. https://www.nytimes.com/2018/04/05 /business/trump-trade-war-china.html.

Patrick W. Watson, "How Trump's Trade Policies Actually Damage The Economy," *Forbes*, December 20, 2018. https:// www.forbes.com/sites/patrickwwatson/2018/12/20 /how-trumps-trade-policies-actually-damage-the-economy /#105138b2441f.

Index